MISADVENTURES
IN BROADCASTING

Zany stories from 50 plus years of
sports play–by–play

RAY GOSS
Foreword by Nellie King

www.raygoss.com

Printed in the United States of America

ISBN: 978-0-9717475-8-6

Printed by
Laurel Valley Graphics
Latrobe, Pennsylvania

CONTENTS

FOREWORD

Ray Goss started broadcasting Duquesne Dukes basketball as a partner with Joe Tucker in 1968 during that year's NIT Tournament. And now, in the year 2008, it can be noted that his 40-year tenure as "The Voice of the Duquesne Dukes Basketball" is the longest continuous association of a radioman with a single team in the entire history of Pittsburgh sports.

A proper impression of the longevity of Ray Goss with Dukes basketball can be realized from the list of coaches and players he has covered. The coaches include Red Manning, John Cinicola, Mike Rice, Jim Satalin, John Carroll, Scott Edgar, Darelle Porter, Danny Nee, and Ron Everhart.

Just as memorable are a host of the Dukes players, people like Norm Nixon, Billy Zopf, Mike Barr, Jarrett Durham, Mickey Davis, Lionel Billingy, the twins Barry and Garry Nelson, Bruce Atkins, Derrrick Alston, Tom Pipkins, Mike James, and Kieron Achara.

Naturally, in the course of this long career, Goss broadcast a great many very exciting games. Among these are the 1968 All-College Tournament in Oklahoma City, an overtime win for the Dukes over Providence at the Civic Arena, and the 1977 Eastern Eight Championship game that sent the Dukes to the NCAA Tournament.

The All-College Tournament featured Pistol Pete Maravich, who scored 54 points in the title game to beat the Dukes 94-91. But possibly Goss's most exciting game was that 81-80 overtime win over Providence at Pittsburgh's Civic Arena. The Friars led 80-79 with eight seconds to play when Norm Nixon got a steal on the in-bounds pass. Dribbling to the top of the circle, he then fired a quick pass to Bernie O'Keefe, who buried the shot from the right corner for a thrilling 81-80 win at the buzzer.

Heading the list of those outstanding opponents who played against the Dukes, besides Pete Maravich of LSU, are Bob Lanier of St. Bonaventure, George Gervin of Eastern Michigan, Spencer Haywood of Detroit, Austin Carr and John Shumate of Notre Dame, and Lamar Odom of Rhode Island.

My association with Ray as his color announcer began in the 1973-74 basketball season. We have worked together nearly thirty years, during a time when many changes, including the shot clock and the three-point shot, created a faster and higher scoring game. I have always been impressed by Ray's ability to follow the often hectic play, and by his consistent, colorful, and accurate description of the game from toss-up to final whistle.

The biggest change in Duquesne basketball occurred during the 1976-77 season when the Dukes joined the Eastern Eight, the first college basketball conference to be formed in the East. The Eastern Eight included, besides Duquesne, Pitt, Penn State, West Virginia, George Washington, Villanova, Massachusetts, and Rutgers. The Dukes were the Cinderella team in the Eastern Eight that initial season. And, with the sparkling, dominating play of Norm Nixon, they brought home the Eastern Eight title, by running off wins over Penn State, Massachusetts, and Villanova at the Spectrum in Philadelphia. Attendance was light in that first year; but the next season, when the year's-end tournament was held at the Civic Arena in Pittsburgh, huge crowds showed up for the games.

It has been a tough roller coaster ride for Ray during those 40 years of radio broadcasting Duquesne basketball. But, because he is clearly a true professional, he has never lost his passion for the game, or for the Dukes; nor has his determination for excellence in his description ever lessened.

It was a real joy and a privilege to have shared so many years with Ray Goss, and to have been privy to so many of his wild experiences. I know you readers of Misadventures in Broadcasting will enjoy very much these stories from his long and rich radio career.

Nellie King

INTRODUCTION

What could be better for a sports fan than going to games and getting paid to attend them? I mean it's usually the other way around: you pay to see them play.

Well, for more than 50 years now 98% of the sporting events I attend each year I'm paid to be there. That's because I'm hired to broadcast these events, usually on the radio, occasionally on TV.

I figure I've broadcast at least 3,000 games in the last half century. And I think I'm being conservative. That works out to about 60 games a year, and there were many years I know I broadcast more. In the 1994–95 basketball season, for example, there were 81 basketball games, to go along with football, baseball, softball, and harness races. So the average those two years was 80 to 85 broadcasts per year.

And with that many games, sometimes things out of the ordinary occur. And that's what this book is all about.

In January, 2005, I was having lunch in Pittsburgh with my good friend Bob Gussin. During the course of the conversation Bob told me that he and his wife Pat had recently started their own publishing company.

"Bob, that's amazing because I've had some interesting experiences over the years in sports broadcasting, and I've written a little about them," I said.

And when I told Bob a couple of the stories he expressed an interest in having me write more. In fact, he told me he wanted to see a manuscript by summer. "No promises," he said. "We have an editorial board, and they would have to approve anything before it gets published."

Well, that was enough to spur me on.

The fact that Bob's editorial board told him if my name had been Bob Costas or John Madden, then they would consider publishing my book, didn't deter me too much. In fact it made me want to make sure this book got published somehow, some way.

And that's when another good friend, Bill Betts, a retired English professor from Indiana University of Pennsylvania, came to my aid.

Bill had taught me as much English as my teachers in high school and college. I can still recall his admonition after hearing me on a high school football broadcast, describing an injured player "laying" on the ground.

"Raymond," Bill said (He always called me "Raymond" when he was going to correct me.) "laying means to place or put; lying means to rest or recline. You need to use the word lying when describing an injured football player who is prostrate on the turf."

That's just one example of how Bill helped me with the correct usage of the English language, and so when it came to trying to write a book, I naturally called upon Bill to correct the many grammatical errors that I knew would invade my writing.

And it was Bill who came up with the title for this book. I originally was going to call it something like "50 Years Behind the Mike," but as soon as Bill suggested "Misadventures in Broadcasting," I knew that at least I had found the right title.

It's been a blast for me to recall the off-beat, unusual, incredible, humorous, and at times embarrassing experiences that have occurred over the last half century while I was broadcasting sporting events throughout the country, and I hope you'll enjoy reading about them as much as I have enjoyed writing about them.

DEDICATION

This book is dedicated to the thousands of announcers who have been there or are doing sports play-by-play on radio stations everywhere. Hopefully they will be able to identify with some of the experiences described in the book.

1

HOW IT ALL STARTED

When he walked into the room, I recognized him immediately. I hadn't seen him in 40, maybe 50 years. After all it was our high school graduating class's 50th anniversary and he really wasn't in our class anyway. He was a year, maybe two ahead.

But Jack Mox hadn't changed much over the years, at least not so much that I wouldn't recognize him, and he obviously knew who I was, for he came directly toward me with right hand outstretched.

Now his wife was a different matter. Patty Davis did graduate with me from Scott Township High school in Carnegie and the woman with Jack was I guess Patty, although I would not have recognized her had she come in alone.

Some people change a lot over the years and Patty's hair had obviously turned color and she was wearing glasses. It's funny how you remember your classmates as they were when you were in high school with them, especially if you see them only at class reunions.

And our 1954 class didn't really get together all that often. We had our first reunion at 15 years, the second at 25, the third at 44 (you figure that one out), and now, the big one, at 50.

Patty was one of I'd say eight to ten girls in high school whom you would definitely take a second or third look at, especially if you were a 16 or 17-year-old boy who was now noticing the opposite sex.

When we greeted each other now, after Jack had shaken my hand, I could appreciate that this was indeed Patty, albeit now 67 and not 17.

Patty and Jack had remained in the Carnegie area, a suburb of Pittsburgh just eight miles away, and Jack immediately started talking sports, remarking that he has heard me many times broadcasting Duquesne basketball on various Pittsburgh radio stations. I told him I was about to begin my 37th year doing the games.

He also remembered the TV sportscasts I had done for a couple of weekends in the '70s on Channel 11 in Pittsburgh, and naturally I related the circumstances behind that, how they had called me and had explained that they just needed someone to fill in for a couple of weekends.

Then he told me of an incident I certainly couldn't remember, but he told it with such conviction and detail that I figured it must be true.

He began by declaring that it certainly didn't surprise him that I had become a sports play–by–play broadcaster. Astonished, I said, "Why?"

"Well," he continued, "I remember vividly one fall day when I along with Murph," and he then rattled off four other boys' names who were all a couple of years older than I, "were playing touch football on Locust Street, and you were standing on the sidewalk watching us."

Locust Street is where I lived and we often played touch football, and other sports right on the street, since there were no playgrounds or fields nearby. The field would extend from telephone pole to telephone pole.

Jack continued. "As we were playing I could hear you starting to do play–by–play. You were probably ten or eleven at the time and you were describing exactly what we were doing."

I interrupted. "You've got to be kidding. I don't remember that at all."

I had probably been too embarrassed and had simply erased the whole experience from my memory bank.

But Jack persisted. "No. I remember it distinctly. It was pretty neat to be hearing my name as we were playing. And that's why it didn't surprise me at all when years later I began hearing you on the radio."

Well, if Jack Mox's memory is that vivid who am I to dispute him?

I then told Jack about my earliest memories of wanting to be a sports broadcaster.

I said it happened a couple of years later when as a member of the Scott Township basketball and baseball squads (but one who not only didn't start, but rarely got into the games) I began to realize that I would never make it as a pro athlete. That's when I started to think about ways I could still be involved in sports, and announcing games seemed like a pretty good idea.

I told Jack it was about then that I realized they had such things as portable radios. Forget transistors. This was long before them. The portable radio I convinced my Dad to buy me was a huge boxlike contraption made by Fada, engineered so ingeniously that when you pulled off the back cover you could insert six big batteries that would convert it to a portable radio, if you could possibly call something that big "portable".

And I remember lugging that Fada radio to Saturday afternoon high school football games and holding it close to my ear as my Dad and I watched the Scott Township football action. There were no such things as headsets back then; at least one didn't come with the Fada radio.

I would then dutifully report to my Dad the score of the current Pitt game or whatever other event was being aired on the radio at the time. And I would be listening to how the play-by-play guys back then called the game, and envisioning how I would do the game if I were calling it.

"Jack," I said, "that's how I remember my first interest in doing sports play-by-play, but your story is much better, and now I know what the first chapter of my book will be."

2

DAGUS MINES

Anyone who has broadcast sports for a small-market radio station as I have for a half-century can regale you with horror stories about getting games on the air.

My all-time all-timer involves a Pennsylvania Senior American Legion baseball inter-district play-off game between Marion Center in Indiana County and Fox Township from Clearfield County.

Two days prior to the game of August 2, 1972, we were informed the game would be played in Dagus Mines, Pa. "Where?" I asked incredulously. Over the years I had done baseball, basketball, and football games in virtually every community in Pennsylvania, but I had no idea where Dagus Mines was. When advised it was north of DuBois and that it was the Old Home Phone Company (I am not making this up) whom we would have to contact in order to install a connection, I called immediately to arrange for a phone line at the field.

Well, I discovered that the Old Home Phone Company could do the job all right given enough time, but the cost of running a line to such a remote site on such short notice was just impossible. There had to be another way.

A phone call to the Fox Township baseball team manager revealed that there were some homes near the playing field, which as it turned out, was a not so finely groomed active cow pasture. The manager produced the name and phone number of a lady he thought would be cooperative and whose home was right near the field. A phone call to the lady brought assurance that we could indeed run some line from her phone to the field.

The game had been scheduled for a Saturday afternoon. I left my radio station headquarters in Indiana, Pa., very early, first to make sure I could find Dagus Mines, and, second, to provide enough time to secure all the line I knew we'd have to string. My eight-year-old son David went with me, for companionship, and to climb whatever trees were required for stringing the line.

We arrived in Dagus Mines without getting lost, about two hours before game time. I promptly called the radio station, collect of course, to alert the staff that we were on site and to advise them to hold on while I unscrewed the mouthpiece on the phone, alligator clipped the leads, ran out to the field where the line was strung and our remote gear hooked up, and checked the line. Alas, after all of that, now no response from the station. Back to the house, some 70 yards away, unfasten the alligator clips, screw on the mouthpiece, and still nothing. Silence. The line was dead.

Called the station again, collect as I remember. "What happened?"

"I don't know," came the reply, "but when you unscrewed the mouthpiece, the line went dead."

Two more attempts. Same results. The conclusion was inescapable. The Old Home Phone Company was ahead of Bell Telephone in one respect. Mess with their mouthpiece and zap, the line goes dead.

And, unfortunately, the phone in the gracious lady's house wasn't even near enough to a window that I could try to call the game from inside the house.

Well, I mused, *at least I can call back reports every half-inning or so.* But of course such reports are nothing compared to the play-by-play account of every pitch.

I sauntered back to the field. Although still nearly an hour remained before game time, I was already resigned to my fate. There were no more houses around and even if there were, my impressions of the Old Home Phone Company had dashed any hopes I had had of successfully unscrewing mouthpieces and running the line.

As I gazed out over the outfield, which was treacherously potted with holes and steeped in high grass, I noticed a house some 50 yards on out beyond the left-field fence. *Hmmm. I wonder?*

Already I was banging on the door. A middle-aged lady appeared. "I don't suppose you have a phone you wouldn't be using the next two hours?"

6

"Why, well, yes we do."

I explained my dilemma and then posed the critical question, "Does the phone happen to be near a window that's facing the field?"

"Well, it's in the dining room. Come see for yourself. Perhaps the cord will reach the window."

The family was just sitting down to a late lunch when I stretched the cord across the dining room table, opened the window, and handed the receiver to my son David.

I hurried outside to see what kind of view I would have. Well, I would not be able to sit down. In fact, I was glad to be six feet two, because I would have to stand erect in order to cradle the phone on my shoulder, and between my ear and mouth. I would need both hands for the field glasses, which, luckily, I had thought to bring, and for the scorebook with which I identified the players and kept the record.

I was in business, albeit a good 475 to 500 feet from home plate.

"Oh," cautioned the lady from the dining room table, "I forgot to tell you, we're on a party line.

"Thanks," I replied dryly, already envisioning the worst.

The game finally got underway. I found I didn't use the field glasses much. The right arm of the umpire told me instantly whether the pitch was a strike. Besides, without binoculars I found it easier to pick up the flight of the ball once it was hit.

But I could not always make out the crack of the bat, for I kept hearing clicks on the line throughout the broadcast. Doubtless these testified to the presence of other parties on the "party" line, but, amazingly, no one ever said anything. If he had, obviously it would have gone right out on the air. Everyone on the line must have appreciated the professional tone of the broadcast and was just glad to be part of history being made this day in Dagus Mines. These were the musings I permitted myself between innings when we were running commercials from the station.

About midway though the game, the lady from the house back near home plate came running out to my broadcast position. "You're supposed to call the station," she informed me.

"What?" Panic. *I'm on the air,* I thought. *I know that. What could*

7

be the problem?

Just then, I heard the Old Home Phone Company operator say, "Sir, I'm sorry. I cut you off temporarily. But you're back on now. No one ever stayed on the line this long and when I heard a pause for a minute (this would be the time allowed for commercials) I assumed you were finished."

We hadn't missed too much, an out or two at most.

About the fifth inning, a pickup truck wheeled into the yard and parked right in line with my view of the field. But when David alerted the driver to the needs of the historic broadcast the driver politely repositioned the truck.

In the seventh, a motorcycle roared in. The rider, when made aware of the situation, came forward with arm extended. "How about a beer, buddy? You look like you could use one."

I smiled and waved him off. There are only two times I don't drink beer—while broadcasting games, and when not broadcasting them.

The rest of the game was rather uneventful.

Fox Township won it, 2-0. The key play occurred in the eighth inning when Mike Betts, Marion Center's left fielder, while going for a routine fly ball, stepped into a hole and disappeared. The ball fell safely, and the game's only runs were tallied.

Now whenever I'm traveling on route 119 North through DuBois heading to a game in Olean, New York, or to a sports event somewhere in northern Pennsylvania, I still smile when I see the sign pointing to the right. "Dagus Mines," it reads, "this way."

3

WEST VIRGINIA VS. CARNEGIE TECH

The main reason I chose to attend Duquesne University was Radio Station WDUQ-FM.

I knew DUQ was student-operated and broadcast not only the Dukes home basketball games but some high school football games and various other sporting events from time to time. What better way to get some actual play-by-play experience than to go to Duquesne, major in Radio-TV Journalism and work at DUQ with the goal of getting to do as much play-by-play as possible before I graduate.

So in my freshman year I started hanging out at DUQ between and after classes and doing the usual mundane things to get some broadcast experience. And eventually I was assigned a couple of small on-air shifts which no one else wanted. In the summer of my freshman year I would bus it to Pittsburgh from my home in Carnegie to work the afternoon shift, which consisted of playing classical LP's, and learning to pronounce such names as Richard Wagner (Ree card Vahg ner) and doing an occasional newscast and sportscast, which consisted of "ripping and reading" copy from the UP newswire.

As a sophomore, thanks to Jim Murphy, who was a senior and Sports Director of WDUQ, I was assigned to go to some games and keep statistics for the announcers. Eventually I was allowed to do the "color" on a couple of games so I could get my "feet wet" on an actual live broadcast.

Then I got my big break; it was my first play-by-play. Jim Murphy let me watch the first half of a Carnegie Tech (now Carnegie Mellon) game so that I could get familiar with the players from both teams. Then as the second half was about to start he said "and now with the play-by-play action here's Ray Goscinski" (my real name before I eventually got it legally changed to Ray Goss).

I remember watching the action, my heart thumping in my chest, as Carnegie Tech came down, passed the ball a couple of times and launched a shot, which missed, and I said nary a word. Finally I blurted out a few syllables, then a couple of words, and finally I began to string some sentences together. I had rehearsed for this moment many times, but it sure was different to actually do it live on the air as opposed to in my own mind.

After a few minutes of stuttering around I'm sure I got somewhat better, but I'm glad no one ever tape-recorded my first effort. Then again everyone has to start somewhere.

At any rate I got through the game and was already looking forward to the next time I'd be called upon to do play-by-play.

That occurred on Jan. 11, 1956 at Skibo Gym on the Carnegie Tech campus. The Tartans were hosting powerful West Virginia. Back then, powerful Division 1 schools would schedule non D1 teams as a matter of course. That season the Mountaineers had walloped Carnegie Tech in West Virginia's home opener 92-79 and weren't expecting to have much difficulty in winning at Skibo. After all WVU had All-American Hot Rod Hundley and 6-10 center Lloyd Sharrar. WVU was coached by the legendary Fred Schaus, who later went on to coach the Lakers in the NBA.

Carnegie Tech had a pretty good team, for its class. Their top players were Alan Frank, their "big man" at 6-3 and hot shooting guard 5-10 Bill Soffa.

It was a terrific game with the home crowd energizing the underdog Tartans. The game came down to the final seconds with Carnegie Tech amazingly holding a 68-65 lead. Hundley, who was spectacular all night, drove for the basket and was fouled. He would have two shots with two seconds left to play. The Mountaineers called time out and the strategy was obvious.

First, some background. Back in 1956 the rules were a bit different than they are now. The free throw lane was only 6 feet wide, and incredibly, the rebound positions gave one man from each team the inside position. This meant that 6-10 Sharrar would be three feet from the basket on the left and Hundley's objective, after making the first free-throw, would be to glance the second attempt off the left side of the rim so that Sharrar could corral the rebound and simply lay it in to tie the game and force overtime.

Hundley did his job perfectly, making the first, cutting WVU's deficit to two, and caroming his second attempt off the left side of the rim. Sharrar went up, uncontested, because he had the inside rebounding position. But instead of grabbing the rebound Sharrar tipped the rebound off the glass. The ball rimmed the basket and popped out right back to Sharrar. He tipped it again and again it went off the glass and in and out of the basket and right back to Sharrar for the third time. Again he tipped it off the glass into the basket to tie the game. But wait, the buzzer had sounded before the third tip and the basket was waved off. Carnegie Tech had completed an astounding upset over West Virginia, 68-66!

In 1956 dunking wasn't allowed or Sharrar could simply have grabbed the rebound and slammed it home to tie the game. Also, and this rule hasn't changed, until the ball is touched after a missed free-throw the clock doesn't start. Two seconds is a lot of time, and Sharrar had plenty of time to grab the rebound and simply lay it back up off the glass. But hindsight is always 20-20 and no doubt Sharrar thought it would be so easy to simply tip it back in off the glass. But two tips went in and out and the game was history.

After this game I was hooked on play-by-play. What an exciting game! And I had the privilege of calling it on the radio. Back then WDUQ was a small student station and I'm sure the listening audience could have been counted on two hands, if even that. But it was a great experience and I couldn't think of anything I'd rather do than broadcast games and eventually get paid for doing them.

It was then I became determined to make play-by-play sports broadcasting my lifetime work.

4

MUSPORT

In 1957 I was a junior at Duquesne University and after my friend Jim Murphy graduated I succeeded him as Sports Director of the student-operated university radio station WDUQ-FM.

Not long after I had been in harness the station received a phone call from Dudey Moore, the legendary head basketball coach of the Dukes. He was asking to talk to whoever was in charge of sports broadcasting at the station. And when the faculty director of the station, B. Kendall Crane, told me that Dudey Moore wanted to see me, I was both flabbergasted and elated.

When I met Dudey he told me that he and a partner, Dr. Al Statti, had started a new business and were looking for some students to work part-time, and since it involved sports, he was approaching WDUQ. After he explained in great detail what the job would mean, I promptly agreed to it. I could appreciate that this kind

DUDEY MOORE
Legendary Duquesne coach whom I got to know when he and Dr. Al Statti started MuSport and Dudey hired me. Here he is at the triumphant aftermath of the Dukes 1955 NIT Title game, when the NIT held as much if not more prestige than the NCAA Championship.

of work would be easy for me and would permit me lots of time for my studies and class preparation.

MuSport was a combination of music and sports, thus the name. The music was contained on large reels and programmed to run continuously. The only interruption occurred when there were sports scores to report. These scores came in via a Western Union ticker, and my job was to announce them by simply pressing a button on the microphone, which muted the music and gave the score. What could be easier?

I didn't ask a lot of questions and as I began the job I found that the clients for the service were basically places in the Pittsburgh area in which sports bettors hung out, in other words, bars and bookie joints. Each day when I reported for work there would be a sheet with a list of the basketball, baseball, or football games scheduled. If a game wasn't on the list, I didn't have to bother giving that score. In other words the sheets were betting sheets.

At first Dudey and I handled most of the shifts but when it came time for basketball practice to begin and he became busier, he asked me to hire some other part-time help, which I did. Dudey would still show up at times and of course to pay me every two weeks.

Saturday afternoons in football season were interesting. Dudey would come in and when some of his friends would show up they would play gin in an adjoining office, coming into my work area occasionally to check the latest scores.

One Saturday as the crew was playing gin and sipping some libations from paper cups, Dr. Statti sauntered in. His dental office was across the hall from the MuSport offices in the Plaza Building in Pittsburgh. Doc was obviously still having office hours on this particular Saturday because he was wearing his white dental garb. He asked me how things were going and went on to join Dudey and his friends. Before I knew it, he was involved in the gin game. I didn't think anything of it until about a half-hour later when a man walked into the office with his white dental bib on and holding his jaw.

"Is Doc Statti in here?" he asked. "My mouth has been numb for some time now."

With that I could hear Doc Statti from the next office, "Ray, tell him to go back to my office. I'll be right there."

A few minutes later Doc Statti emerged from the gin game and headed back to his patient.

Saturday nights during basketball season were interesting. People would show up to check the scores, and it was apparent they had more than a fan's interest in the outcome of the games. When their team was leading I would get "Atta boy Ray." But when their team was losing, it was "Ray, you're not doing me any good tonight," as if I had something to do with what transpired on various courts around the nation.

I distinctly remember a phone call one of the regulars made late one Saturday night. His end of the conversation went something like this, "Yea, I'm down ten in New York, but I'm up six in Chicago, and the west coast games aren't in yet." Ten of course meant ten thousand, etc.

One of the regulars at MuSport was Gene Dargan. I liked Gene because he took an interest in me and would bring me burgers from the White Tower Restaurant downstairs.

But I didn't know too much about Gene, mainly because I guess I didn't want to. Gene was a big guy, close to 300 pounds, and someone had told me he was a wrestling promoter.

One day when I arrived at MuSport for my evening shift, I got quite a shock. As was my habit, I picked up a copy of the evening *Pittsburgh Press* only to discover that the front-page story was providing details about a shooting and murder that occurred in a Pittsburgh suburban auto dealership. As I read the story, the name Gene Dargan jumped out at me. Gene, the story said, was a witness to the shooting. As I started to read more of the details, the office door opened, and there was Gene Dargan standing there.

I'll never forget his words as he saw me reading the front page of the Press.

"Ray," he said, "don't believe everything you read in the paper."

In addition to getting paid and being able to keep up with my studies, MuSport also helped me stay in good physical shape.

In basketball season I would have to wait until the west coast scores were final before I could sign off. Since the games started at eight p. m. west coast time, it would be 11 o'clock in the east and one a. m. before the finals came in. After giving the final west coast scores, I would hurriedly lock the office, take the elevator to the street floor and begin running. You see the bus to Carnegie left at 1:15 a. m. from Horne's, which was at least a mile away. So I would run through the streets of Pittsburgh at one a. m., amazingly never once missing my bus or being stopped by one of Pittsburgh's finest.

Now as I look back on those days in the 1950s I can't help thinking that if MuSport existed today, what would the NCAA say about Dudey Moore's involvement in such an enterprise?

And what would happen if a reporter found out about MuSport, which would not have been difficult? Why he would have a sensational story that headlined a Division 1 basketball coach's association with known bookies and high stake bettors.

Of course there was never anything out of the way about Dudey Moore back then.

The 1950s. It certainly was a different era.

5

SNEAKING INTO THE FINAL FOUR

The 1966 NCAA Finals were scheduled for the University of Maryland in College Park and I wanted to go.

Carl Kologie was the Sports Editor of *The Indiana Gazette* at the time and in addition to my on-air duties at WDAD in Indiana I also doubled as the Sports Director and play-by-play guy for basketball, football, and anything else that came along.

I called Carl and asked him whether he would like to go to the games and whether he thought we could get press passes for the Final Four since we were both members of the media. "It's worth a shot," was his reply.

CARL KOLOGIE
Fellow Duquesne graduate. He and Mossie Murphy in the mid '50s, became the first cheerleaders for the Dukes' basketball team.

So we wrote to the NCAA headquarters in Kansas several weeks before the games and when we didn't hear anything, we started to call about our requests. We were told they couldn't be sure we would get credentials because they had to honor so many requests and naturally they favored the bigger media outlets. We were told we may or may not get media passes but the only way to know for sure was to check at the game site the day before or the day of the first game.

Because Carl had another connection that might be able to help us if the media passes didn't materialize, we decided to chance it and head for College Park. Carl had a friend named Bud Apple, who was in charge of maintenance at Cole Field House, the site of the games. To Carl's appeal Bud said he *might* be able to get us into the field house, but insisted there was no guarantee.

We also knew that Herm Sledzik, the coach of the IUP basketball team, was going to the Final Four and when we contacted him he said he planned to drive to Maryland by himself, and it would certainly be better if we all traveled together, which we did.

The pairings for the semi-finals pitted Kentucky against Duke in the first game and Texas Western versus Utah in the nightcap. An hour before the first game Carl and I checked to see whether we had media credentials. Carl did and I didn't. Herm, meanwhile, was to get his ticket from his old basketball coach at Penn State, John Egli. So it appeared that two of us would get to see the games and that I would be relegated to listening to them on the radio. But that's when Carl's friend Bud Apple stepped in to offer his help.

We had met Bud shortly after arriving in College Park and he had said that if we needed his help we were to call him, which Carl did. Carl reported to me that Bud would meet me outside the south gate 15 minutes before the start of the first game. "Okay," I said. What choice did I have?

So as Carl and Herm proceeded to enter Cole File House I was left standing outside with a transistor radio listening to the pre-game show and wondering whether Bud would show up at all, and would he be able to get me into the games.

Just as I was giving up hope, Bud showed up. It was ten minutes before tip-off. Donning his Maryland baseball cap, he said, "Follow me."

When he knocked on the door at the south gate and no one came, he knocked a bit louder. Finally the door opened and a man wearing NCAA credentials asked Bud what he wanted.

Without hesitation, Bud replied, "I'm in charge of maintenance here and I need to go upstairs to check something."

The NCAA man looked Bud over warily, and I thought *we're doomed*. But then he said, "I recognize you. Okay, but don't go into the field house itself."

"No problem," Bud said, "I just need to check on something, and oh, by the way, he's with me."

Like that's going to work I thought, but the NCAA official said, "Okay. Remember, though, you're not allowed into the field house without a ticket." I nodded in agreement.

Well, at least we are inside I thought as I could hear but not see the crowd or the floor. *But what good is this going to do me?* I reflected. Bud didn't say much just, "Follow me."

We walked up several flights of stairs to the top of Cole Field House and then Bud edged over toward one of the ushers who were guarding doors that would lead into the Field House. He whispered something to him and the guy motioned to me to come in. In parting, Bud tossed off a "Good luck," and disappeared.

So there I was, high above the floor just as the first game was about to begin. I didn't have a seat of course because I didn't have a ticket. Since no one else was standing I started to worry that someone would want to see my ticket and that in no time at all I'd be back outside.

I have to get a seat I thought. But where? The games are a complete sell-out. As I looked way down near the floor I could see where all the media were seated, including my friend Carl Kologie, who was in the first row, practically at mid-court. Then I noticed something else. Not all the media seats were occupied. I figured, well, they were in the media room getting some last-minute snacks or drinks and would be in their seats shortly. I'd better wait before I try to occupy one of those seats.

So I watched the first four or five minutes of the Kentucky-Duke game from peanut heaven. During a time-out I decided to make my move.

As I began the long walk down through the stands, fortunately no one stopped me, and as confident as I could be, even though I was shaking in my boots, I strolled to an open seat and plunked myself down at a position that was reserved for a newspaper from a town in the state of Indiana. I can't recall the name of the town, but I thought *well, I live in Indiana, Indiana, Pa., that is.*

While the game continued, no one showed up to throw me out even though I wasn't wearing any credentials. As the first game progressed, then the second, I relaxed more and even began enjoying the action. I didn't dare venture toward the media room or frankly anywhere for fear that someone would notice I wasn't wearing any credentials.

As expected, Kentucky won the first game; but unheralded Texas Western captured the second contest.

Later that night when Carl, Herm, and I met up at the dorm where we were staying on the Maryland campus, courtesy of Carl's friend Bud, I relished reliving my story on how I had sneaked into the games.

Then Herm told us a story that rivaled mine.

When he had gone to get his ticket at "will call," he found a message reporting that his contact, John Egli, had already gone into the Field House and that he had Herm's ticket with him.

Herm thought, well that's no problem. I'll just tell the ticket taker the story and I'm sure he'll let me in. But while Herm was waiting in line to get into the game, he perceived that the man in front of him was having quite a discussion with the ticket taker.

It seemed that because this man did not have a ticket he was not about to get into the Field House. Herm listened as the man pleaded, "You don't understand. I'm Tommy Harmon with CBS and I'm working the game, and I need to get in." The ticket taker would have none of that: "I don't care who you are, you're not getting in without a ticket."

Herm thought *if he won't let Tommy Harmon in without a ticket and he should know who he is he's certainly not going to let me in.*

So Herm made a bold move. While the two were arguing, he simply made an end run and walked around both of them, and no one stopped him. He met up with John Egli, who then gave Herm his tickets for both Friday's and Saturday's games.

Carl was the only one who didn't have a hair-raising tale to tell, but he enjoyed hearing about our incredible experiences.

On Saturday I still faced the prospect of sneaking in again. But Herm's story gave me an idea. "Herm," I said, "you still have your ticket from Friday night, don't you?"

"Yeah, Ray, why?"

"Well, I think I might be able to use it to get in tonight," I said. I didn't want to have to rely on Bud again. Of course if I had to, I would.

"Here it is, Ray. Good luck." Herm was half laughing as he handed me the ticket. The Friday and Saturday game tickets were identical, except for one thing, the date.

While I waited outside Cole Field House, with the crowd filing in for the finals, I considered how I might take advantage of the situation.

I carefully surveyed the ticket-takers. I tried to assess which one was least likely to catch the wrong date on the ticket I was about to hand him. After all, I figured, who possibly would have a Friday night ticket on Saturday since both nights were complete sell-outs.

After about five minutes of observation I made my choice. Then I waited patiently until a group of people approached my selected guy. I melted in with the crowd and the ticket-taker never even glanced at my ticket as he handed me the stub. I was into the finals for the second night and headed right to my seat from the night before, on media row courtside.

Fortunately no one checked me for credentials, and little did I know at the time but the Texas Western-Kentucky game would turn out to be "one for the ages." The Miners were big underdogs against the mighty Wildcats, coached by the legendary Adolph Rupp. But the Don Haskins-coached Miners, who started five blacks (something unheard of in major college basketball in the '60s), outclassed the Wildcats and won in a huge upset, 72-65. The game was later chronicled in Frank Fitzpatrick's book *And the Walls Came Tumbling Down*, as the "Game that changed American sports."

Coming during the civil rights movement in the United States, the win accelerated the recruitment of black basketball players throughout the country, especially in the south.

Following the game I figured why not try to attend the post-game interviews. What could they do to me now if I was turned away from the media interviews? Throw me out? The games were over. No problem again. The media representatives streamed into a large interview room, and I was right in the midst of them.

When Adolf Rupp came to the podium and made some rather brief remarks about the game, it was obvious after the disappointing loss that he wanted to be out of there as soon as possible, or even quicker.

The floor was open for questions for Rupp. Surprised that no one responded immediately, I raised my hand.

The man in charge pointed to me, and I said, "Coach, do you think Bobby Joe Hill was the best point guard you faced this season?"

Hill had been the spark plug for Texas Western. He scored a game-high 20 points and handled the ball flawlessly in directing the Miners' attack. In my estimation, he was simply sensational and without a doubt the star in the championship game.

I'll never forget Rupp's response. "Well," he said, "I wouldn't say he was the best point guard we faced this season. He would be one of them, but we played against some pretty good guards this year."

I was disappointed. I thought he could have given Hill a little more credit.

The next day, though, I was pleased to read the response to my question in write-ups in the local newspapers.

I've often thought about that Final Four in 1966. I'm sure that with the additional security in place now there's no way I would be able to do what I did. And I hope that now, more than 40 years later, I don't get into any trouble for revealing the fact that I sneaked into the Final Four, not once, but twice.

6

WHAT ABOUT TOM

After searching for several months following my graduation from Duquesne University in Pittsburgh in June, 1958, I received my first job offer at WDAD in Indiana, Pa. And it didn't take me long to accept.

Joe Termin was the General Manager of WDAD and when he called me to offer the job as the "morning man," he said I might want to think about using a different name on the air. He said that if I wanted to use my real name of Ray Goscinski that was okay with him, but it might be easier if I changed or shortened it for on–air use.

He said as Goss was a familiar name in Indiana County I might want to consider it, but whatever I decided was all right with him. Because it was on a Friday when he phoned me at my home in Carnegie, Pa., I had the whole weekend to ponder this momentous decision. I decided to go with Joe's decision and become Ray Goss and call my morning show "Get Up with Goss." I have always liked alliteration.

By and by I met, dated, and eventually married Dorothy Lance of Indiana on October 1, 1960, and we became Dorothy and Ray Goscinski. Meanwhile, I was still Ray Goss on the radio and as I got to know people in Indiana, they got to know me as Ray Goss, not Ray Goscinski.

Then the children started coming along. First, Christine, then, Lisa, David, Tom, and Julie. Jason and Amy would come later. And when they went to school their last name was Goscinski, of course.

Some interesting things happen when you're known by two names. Dee became a member of the Junior Women's Civic Club of Indiana, and was working on a committee with several other women. One day when Dee was grocery shopping she bumped into one of these women and began chatting with her. When Dee realized the other woman didn't seem to know who she was, she thought she'd help her by saying, "I don't think you remember me, I'm Dorothy Goscinski and we met at a Junior Women's Civic Club meeting."

Startled, the other woman blurted out, "Oh, and here I thought you were married to Ray Goss."

Dee then had to explain that she indeed was married to Ray Goss but that Goss was his radio name. "His real name was Goscinski."

Then when our daughter Lisa was in the third grade I remember looking over her shoulder to check some homework she was doing. The first thing I noticed was her name at the top of the paper. It was Lisa Goss. I looked at her, pointed to the name, and said, "Lisa, that's not your name."

And she looked at me with her big, expressive hazel eyes and replied, "But Dad, it's so much easier."

It was after incidents like these two that I thought it would simplify our family's lives if I just went ahead and legally changed our name to Goss.

I decided to do it in the summer so that our children could start the school year fresh in the fall with their new last name. So on July 19, 1971, by order of the Court of Common Pleas of Indiana County, our family's name officially went from Goscinski to Goss.

I had to appear in court to have this accomplished, a simple matter according to my attorney, Bob Douglass. The Honorable Judge Edwin M. Clark was presiding. It so happened that that day there were some criminal proceedings scheduled for court, but Judge Clark said he would take care of my name-change petition first.

I had to be sworn in and with a large audience of lawyers, spectators, and others awaiting their turn before the judge, my case was ready to be heard. Judge Clark began by saying that he knew me and that this was a mere formality. He asked my lawyer to proceed with his questions for me.

Bob Douglass asked a few simple questions designed to make sure my motives for changing my name didn't involve anything illicit like trying to avoid creditors, etc. He asked me my wife's name and birth-date. Then he inquired about my children, saying, "Mr. Goss, would you be so kind as to tell the court your children's names and their dates of birth?"

Whoa, I thought, *I didn't know he was going to ask me that.* But I gathered myself, thinking, I know this, and began.

"Well, first there's Christine Ann, born September, 12th, 1961; then Lisa Marie, November 29th, 1962; David Charles, January 26th, 1964: and Julie Lynn, March 9th, 1970."

That's when I stopped and panicked. That's four children, but we have five. There was a long pause in the courtroom before my attorney prompted me with, "What about Tom?"

"Right," I swallowed hard, "Thomas Edward, born September 30th, 1968."

After the proceeding as I walked out of the court, one of the attorneys present, whom I knew, said, "Boy that's something, don't even know how many kids you have." Naturally he was joking, but now I know what it feels like to be on the stand in front of the court with the pressure on.

When our youngsters went back to school in the fall, there were some teachers who thought that perhaps over the summer there had been a divorce because they now had new names, but, outside of a little confusion like that, the longer it went the easier it became for everyone in our family to be Gosses and not Goscinskis.

Of course there have been many times I wished I had chosen an easier name. At the time I thought what could be easier than Goss. I was used to having my Polish name of Goscinski being butchered throughout my life. There was one notable exception in college when the last name of Goscinski served me well.

It was my senior year at Duquesne University and one of my courses was Elements of Economics, which was taught by Sigmund Lehoczky, a recent arrival in the states from Poland.

Roll call in his class consumed more time than usual because Professor Lehoczky had more than a little difficulty pronouncing a lot of names, but not mine.

As he called the roll, he would have to be corrected time and again by students with rather ordinary sounding names, at least by American standards. But when he came to my name, no problem, he would say it loud and clear, giving it the full Polish pronunciation, "Gohsh-shteen'skee" instead of "Go-sin'skee," the Anglicized version.

One time when he came to my classmate Beth Riley, he was trying his best, but all that was coming out was "Rrrr'ill." After a couple of attempts with no response from anyone, I realized that Beth didn't know he was calling her name. "Beth," I whispered to her two rows away, "it's you." She then responded to get Professor Lehoczky off the hook.

Naturally I got an "A" in Elements of Economics.

But that was the only time I can recall where it was an advantage to be named Goscinski, so when I readily agreed to start using the name "Goss," I figured, how could anyone have trouble with a name that simple?

How indeed! I can't begin to count the times on the phone I have to spell it out for someone by emphasizing the "ss" and saying "as in Sam." Or how many times I've received mail addressed to Ray Goff.

I quickly realized that on the phone, even though I think I have pretty good diction as a result of my radio background, an "s" sounds like an "f." But the best one happened recently when I was on the phone with the athletic director's office of a high school. I was scheduled to broadcast a game involving their school and was asking the secretary to fax me a copy of the football roster. I dutifully spelled out my last name, saying "s" as in Sam. When the fax arrived, it came to Ray Gosf.

It's times like that when I think I might have been better off just sticking with Goscinski.

7

MY BIG BREAK

I went to college because I wanted to be a sports broadcaster, and not just someone who read the sports or reported it, but someone who did play-by-play. That seemed to me to be much more interesting and exciting than just reporting sports. Of course I knew I might also have to do sports reporting to get started but my primary goal was to do play-by-play and naturally I wanted to do it at the highest level, if not on the networks, at least in a major market, like Pittsburgh, where I was born and raised.

I also knew it was tough to start at the top and that most likely I would have to start at a small-town station to gain the experience I needed to impress the big-wigs who did the hiring in the major markets.

So I was delighted when I started working at WDAD in Indiana, Pa., in November of 1958. Not only because it was my first full-time job in radio as the morning man with my "Get Up with Goss" show, but also because WDAD carried local sports and I would be their play-by-play guy.

Since I had attended Duquesne University, where basketball was the number one sport, I always envisioned my ideal job, at least until I hit the networks, as doing play-by-play on Duquesne Dukes basketball. So as I honed my play-by-play skills, doing at first Indiana State Teachers College (later to become Indiana State College and then Indiana University of Pennsylvania) basketball and football, plus Indiana High football and various other local sporting events, I was always looking to take the next step.

EARL BUNCHER
General Manager of NBC–owned WJAS in Pittsburgh who in 1968 hired me to broadcast the Duquesne basketball games. A terrific guy who later produced the Duquesne games for Action Communications. We never had any problems and I have the greatest respect for Earl.

Duquesne basketball's fortunes took a down turn in the mid '60s, so much so that the games were no longer even on the radio in Pittsburgh. Then in the '67-'68 season the Dukes started winning again, and as the end of the season approached I felt certain they would at least get a bid to the NIT Tournament in New York. So I made sure that in addition to attending some home games when my schedule permitted, I expressed interest in broadcasting the Duquesne games in the NIT should the team receive a bid.

Well, they did get the bid and I was promptly in touch with Clair Brown, the Sports Information Director at Duquesne. He in turn put me in touch with Bud Stevenson, a Pittsburgh advertising executive with Vic Maitland Associates, and someone who was interested in lining up sponsors for the broadcasts.

Long story short, the Duquesne games in the NIT in 1968 would be carried on WWSW in Pittsburgh with Joe Tucker, a well known veteran sports broadcaster, and me doing the games. Joe had broadcast Pittsburgh Steelers football on radio and TV and Duquesne basketball for years. In fact I got to know him as a student at Duquesne when I would be broadcasting the Dukes' games from the Pitt Field House on WDUQ, the Duquesne student-operated

JOE TUCKER
Legendary Pittsburgh sports announcer who broadcast the Pittsburgh Steelers football games from 1936 to 1967.

station, and Joe would be airing the games on WWSW. He always treated me cordially and I was delighted when Bud Stevenson called me with the arrangements on the trip to New York to do the NIT games.

The three of us, Joe, Bud, and I, flew into the Big Apple on March 16th. The next day we were watching the St. Patrick's Day Parade and then headed to Madison Square Garden for the Dukes opening round game with Fordham. Bud was the producer of the broadcast, but he deferred to Joe Tucker, the veteran, when he asked him, "Well, Joe, how do you want to handle the on-air duties?"

Without hesitation, Joe responded, "Well Ray and I will split the play-by-play. I'll do the first half and Ray can do the second, if that's okay with you, Ray?"

"Fine," I said. I couldn't have asked for more.

The broadcast went well except for one thing. The Dukes lost 69-60 to Fordham; so it was "one and done" and before you knew it we were back on the plane to Pittsburgh.

Fast forward ahead to next basketball season. Even though I had only one game under my belt in the Pittsburgh market, I was hopeful that would be enough to land the full-time play-by-play job for the Dukes should the complete schedule be carried on the radio again. Joe Tucker was winding down an illustrious broadcast career and was ready to retire and really I felt I had the inside track, but it's never that easy.

Radio Station WJAS moved into the picture and began negotiating with Duquesne to carry the games. WJAS was NBC owned and operated at the time and they had an all news and talk format and felt sports would tie in nicely with what they were doing. Earl Buncher was the General Manager of WJAS and through my contact at Duquesne, Clair Brown, I was in touch with Earl and began lobbying him for the job.

It came right down to the wire as the season was about to start and still there was no deal with WJAS to air the games. Earl was busily trying to sell enough sponsors to justify carrying the games. He knew I had done the one Duquesne game the previous year but told me sponsors would say "who?" when he told them whom he had planned to hire to do the broadcasts. Some of the sponsors were looking for someone who was better known in the Pittsburgh market and, let's face it, one game on the air didn't exactly make me a household name.

Earl noted that there was one major sponsor, Peoples Gas, who wanted to hear a tape of one of my games. So I sent Earl a reel-to-reel tape of an Indiana State College game. This was before cassettes had come into popularity.

Amazingly, the man at Peoples making the decision, Abe Hays, told Earl after hearing the tape, "He'll do fine."

The first three games of the season came and went with the Dukes winning all three at home, including two in the annual Steel Bowl Tournament, the final over cross-town rival Pitt. That must have been enough to spur an additional sponsor or two because the Monday after the Pitt win Earl called me at WDAD to ask, "How would you like to do the play-by-play on Duquesne basketball?"

I remember my reply, "Sure, what do you think I've been bugging you about all this time?"

I was delighted as Earl explained to me the arrangements and noted when the next game would be, which of course I knew.

After the call from Earl, I quickly called my wife Dee with the exciting news. Now came the tough part.

I had been the General Manager of WDAD for less than two years and we were working hard to begin making some money, obviously something my owner, W. K. Ulerich, was interested in having us achieve.

I knew if I called W. K. to get his permission to do the Duquesne basketball games in Pittsburgh that he would no doubt try to talk me out of it. After all, what was more important, doing a few basketball games, or managing a radio station full-time? I could hear his logical tone already. So I decided that if you want something badly enough you don't ask permission. You just tell your boss, as in this case, what you're going to do and let the chips fall where they may.

The way to do this I figured was with a carefully worded letter, which I immediately began to write.

Basically what I said was that doing the games would enhance my stature in the Indiana area because I would now also be a major market broadcaster. Besides the home games were at night, meaning I didn't have to miss any work; so that wouldn't be a problem. Then I actually counted the number of days and half days I would miss because of the road games and it came out to 11 and a half days. I volunteered to have those days count against my two weeks' vacation, so in essence I wouldn't be missing any work at all. At least that's the way I pitched it and it must have worked because W. K. never responded or called to try to talk me out it.

Thus began my Duquesne basketball play-by-play career that has spanned 40 consecutive years as of this writing, and counting, and a dream come true.

8

THE TROCADERO

I was in my first year as General Manager of WDAD in Indiana, Pa. when I received a phone call from Dick Sharbaugh, Publicity Director for the Meadows Race Track in Washington, Pa.

I had known Dick when he was the Sports Information Director at Duquesne University in the late 50s when I was a student there.

Dick told me about a promotional program the Meadows had instituted and asked me whether I would like to make some extra money. "Sure Dick," I said, "it depends on what it is though."

Dick then explained that to keep harness racing at the Meadows in front of the public during the off season, they would have parties sponsored by organizations throughout the Pittsburgh area. At these parties they would screen films of races from the Meadows. To make it interesting, the people would bet, usually $2.00 a race, the proceeds of which would usually go to a local charity or church.

And here's the kicker. Prior to the party, the Meadows would get the names of the attendees at the party, and instead of calling the horses by name, each horse would be named after someone in attendance.

There were usually eight races and a field of eight horses in each race. So number one in race one might be Joe Jones, number two Harry Smith, etc. And naturally, if you're an attendee, you'll probably put $2.00 on your named horse. It was all in fun, Dick explained, and the charity or church would benefit.

I remember my first question to Dick after he explained the basics. "Is it legal, Dick?"

"Well, Ray," he replied, "bingo isn't exactly legal but churches and firemen hold them all the time and because the money goes to charity, no one really cares."

It wasn't the answer I was looking for, but Dick persisted. "I'm the only one calling these races, Ray, and I need help. I have to turn down bookings for most Saturday nights and that's where you come in. I'm calling some races Saturday night at the Elks right there in Indiana at seven o'clock. Why don't you meet me there and you'll see how it's done?"

I thought, *What the heck. I'll check it out. What do I have to lose?*

So I went and watched. Everyone seemed to be enjoying himself or herself and Dick did an excellent job. He showed me how he did it. He had eight films and he would randomly select one for race number one. He also had 3 x 5 cards that corresponded to each race and showed the progress of the races by number and which numbered horse had won. He would then get his sheet for the first race with the names of the participants and be all set to call the race.

Naturally he would urge the patrons to place their bets, giving them a countdown to post time. Then he'd start the projector and it was "They're off and racing."

Afterwards he asked me whether I felt I could do it, and I said, "I don't see why not," meanwhile completely forgetting about the legality issue. I guess I was caught up in the excitement and the possibility of making some extra money doing something I knew I could do.

Early the next week Dick called me to ask whether I was available that Saturday night. I said, "Sure," and I had my first gig.

For the next three months I was calling races once and sometimes twice a week, and usually getting $50 a night, not bad back in 1967.

Then came the night I called the races at the Trocadero, a night club south of Pittsburgh. I remember my reaction when I walked in and was met by my contact. He showed me where to set up and had everything well organized. I was impressed but also wary because usually I'm the one who has to tell everyone how it's going to work, how the bets are handled, the payoffs, etc. But these people had that all covered, which was good, but much different from what I was accustomed to.

When I spotted a sign on the wall that said the proceeds from the races would benefit the local Catholic Church, I immediately felt better.

The night went off without a hitch. Everything went smoothly, much more so than any other races I had done.

When I finished and started to pack up my tapes and projector I noticed a lot of activity in the room. It looked as though I had been the preliminary act to the main event that was about to begin. People were busy rolling out roulette wheels and other games of chance.

I headed home and didn't give it another thought until Monday morning when I received a call from Dick Sharbaugh. He said, "I guess you heard what happened after you left the Trocadero Saturday night."

"No," I said.

"Well," Dick continued, "the cops raided the place and 37 people were hauled in, fingerprinted, and charged with illegal gambling."

My heart sank to my toes.

"But don't worry, Ray," Dick continued. "I did have to give the cops your name and how to get in touch with you. I don't expect anything to come of it, but if you are questioned, just tell them you don't know anything about any betting on the races."

Don't know anything, I thought, when I'm saying "Place your bets on race number one, only two minutes to post time."

After the phone call, all I could think was, if I get charged, the news will hit *The Indiana Gazette*, and my career as a radio station manager in Indiana will be over. I knew what my boss would do.

I called Dee to tell her of my plight and naturally she was as frightened as I was.

I didn't have long to worry though. It wasn't a half-hour after the call from Sharbaugh that Jacquie Watkins, our receptionist, buzzed me and said there were two gentlemen here to see me, but they wouldn't say who they were. I told Jacquie to send them in.

They introduced themselves and showed me their police ID's, just as they do on TV. When they asked me how the races were handled, I didn't hesitate. I just spilled my guts (they didn't even have to torture me) and told them everything. They were particularly interested in the betting and how it worked.

When I had answered all their questions, one of them said, "Well, Mr. Goss, we know you've been truthful with us because we were both there the whole evening."

Thank goodness I didn't take Dick Sharbaugh's advice and try to stonewall them.

Then I was told that since I wasn't arrested Saturday night, the only thing that might happen is I might be subpoenaed and that would probably come in the form of a registered letter. They explained that the raid was targeted to hit the heavy duty gambling that occurred after my preliminary act.

"If you don't hear anything in about a week, you'll probably be in the clear," I was told.

"But Mr. Goss, do you realize that what you were doing, calling those races where betting was involved, is illegal?"

"I do now," was my immediate reply.

The next week I spent waiting for Dee to call me each day as soon as the mail came to tell me whether I had been subpoenaed.

After about two weeks of "no news was good news," I finally began breathing normally again.

Then Dick Sharbaugh called. He wanted to know whether I would call some races that Saturday night. My response was quick, "You've got to be kidding. No way Dick. I could have lost my job after that Trocadero experience."

"But Ray," Dick went on, "we checked this one out and it's fine. There will be no problems and from now on we'll be more careful so that there won't be any more Trocaderos."

"Dick, all I can say, is thanks, but no thanks."

And what did I learn from all this? No, it's not "Never look a gift horse in the mouth."

Thinking back to the two undercover cops who questioned me, it's more like thank goodness my parents taught me that "Honesty is always the best policy."

9

AIR BENEDICT

Following the regular season in 1989, Indiana University of Pennsylvania made the Division II football play-offs and was scheduled to play Grand Valley State of Michigan on the road in the first game.

Jack Benedict, our Sports Director at 1160 WCCS in Indiana, Pa., said he thought he could line up a flight to Michigan on the morning of the game. That would allow us to broadcast our regularly scheduled Friday night high school football game.

JACK BENEDICT

Jack started doing games with me in 1969 and we worked together through 1994. When you count all of the basketball, football, and baseball games we did, Jack easily tops the list as having done the most games with me, approximately 1,000.

I said, "Go ahead, Jack, see what you can do."

Jack contacted Ken Ciroli, who worked as an engineer at WIUP, IUP's student radio station. Ken was also a licensed pilot and said he could rent a twin-engine plane and would be glad to fly us to Michigan gratis as long as we covered the cost of the flight.

Jack was able to line up three other people so that we could fill the plane and split the cost, making the flight financially feasible.

Early on a Saturday morning we met at the Jimmy Stewart Airport in Indiana and boarded the little six-seat twin-engine prop plane. It was snowing already in Pennsylvania and the forecast wasn't great for Michigan, but Ken Ciroli, the pilot, said we shouldn't have any difficulty.

The first couple of hours of the flight were uneventful except for the fact that we were bucking a pretty strong headwind as we flew west, and we weren't making very good time.

Then as we got into the state of Michigan and neared Grand Rapids the snow got heavier and we seemed to be going even slower. That's when it happened!

The engine on the right sputtered and the plane started tilting to the right.

I was sitting in the co-pilot's seat and I noticed that the needles on the dials in front of me were flipping all over the place. I looked at the pilot and Ken seemed to be making adjustments and talking animatedly to the tower, wherever that was.

Then things got worse, much worse.

The right engine conked out completely and the plane was not only tilting to the right, but dropping, and it seemed to be all over the sky. Besides, the left engine was beginning to sputter.

I put my left hand on the back of the pilot's seat just so I wouldn't get bounced around more, even though I had my seat belt securely fastened.

I looked back at our other four passengers. Jack Benedict was seated directly behind the pilot. Larry Panaia, a former IUP football player and President of the IUP Alumni, was seated directly behind me. Behind Larry was Carl Kologie, who was covering the game for *The Indiana Gazette*, and across from Carl was Joe Wojcik, a photographer for the IUP student newspaper *The Penn*. It was Joe's first flight.

The thing I remembered when I looked around was that eight of the four passengers' eyes were as big as saucers and it didn't take a mind reader to realize what everyone was thinking, *"We're about to buy the farm."*

Then I noticed blood trickling from Jack Benedict's nose. He had some tissues as he tilted his head back to try to stop the bleeding. Later Jack told me that the air vent was bothering him, not to mention the fact we might be heading for a crash landing.

Behind Jack, Joe Wojcik suddenly grabbed the barf bag and the sounds emanating from him were unmistakable. I wondered, since it was Joe's first flight, if he'd ever fly again, then promptly wondered if any of us would ever fly again.

For what seemed to be the next 20 or 30 minutes (really no more than two or three minutes) the plane continued to cascade all over the sky. The right engine was still out and the left engine continued to sputter. No one said a word. But the pilot was saying a lot, and hopefully, was getting life-saving instructions from whomever he was talking to. He kept fingering the different dials and buttons and I knew everyone was certain that "this was it."

I can recall that on looking out all I could see was snow and thinking if we could somehow land on the snow without tipping over, maybe, just maybe we'd simply slide to a stop.

Jack later told me he was hoping we would find a clump of trees and somehow manage to land on top of them to help break our rapid descent.

One thing was certain. We were losing altitude and the plane although still upright was precariously close to flipping over completely. We couldn't have been more than a couple of hundred yards from the ground when all of a sudden the left engine quit sputtering and started to whir as it was supposed to. And, amazingly, the right engine kicked in and after sputtering a bit, it too was back in operation. The plane quit bouncing and began to fly as smoothly as ever. And as Ken made a left turn, there was the airport dead ahead, albeit snow-covered, but the runway was well marked and in another two minutes we landed perfectly as if nothing out of the ordinary had transpired.

As we exited the plane it was obvious that we were at least in a semi-state of shock, but thankful to be on the ground, and more importantly, alive!

I remember saying to Ken, "Boy, that was sure scary."

And Ken replied, "Oh, we were never in any trouble."

I didn't believe it then and I don't today.

At any rate we were on the ground. Now we had to get our rental car to get to the game. Even though he wanted to see the game, Ken said he'd stay behind to get the plane checked out so that it would be sure to be okay for our flight back after the game.

We were running late. It was already 11:30 and the game was slated for a noon kickoff. The car we got was a big Lincoln Continental. I jumped behind the wheel as everyone else piled in. Naturally the roads were snow-covered and treacherous. And we were in a hurry with a rear-wheel drive car. More than once the car fishtailed as I tried to control it and still make it to the game on time.

Once we arrived at the field we were able to convince someone at the game that we had to get as close to the press box as possible. As I drove toward the back of the press box, the Grand Valley team was just re-entering the field and some of their players were blocking our path. I beeped the horn several times. Most of the players moved out of the way, but not number 44. I came within inches of clipping him and had to swerve to the right as he finally leaped out of the way, shouting at me something I'm glad I didn't hear.

As soon as we parked, Jack and I jumped out and hustled to the press box. It was already 11:45, our scheduled air-time and I could just imagine what our people back at the station were thinking. They hadn't heard a word from us.

We found out quickly where our broadcast position was and Jack started hurriedly to set up the equipment as I phoned the station. I told them we had had some trouble, a slight understatement, but that we were here and we'd call them back in about five minutes, ready to go on the air.

We got on just in time for the kick-off. It was a terrific game with IUP carving out a 34-24 victory, posting its first ever play-off victory and thus enabling the team to advance to the national semifinals.

After the game we headed back to the airport. Ken told us that the plane had checked out, and he said, "If you're ready to go, we'd better do it now. There's a patch of blue up there, but if we wait too long we will probably have to stay over and fly back tomorrow morning."

I remember that we all looked at each other. There certainly wasn't an enthusiastic "Let's go." It was more like a reluctant, "Well, let's give it a shot."

We took off and once we leveled off it wasn't but a minute before the right engine started to sputter. I'm sure everyone thought *Here we go again.*

Ken quickly made a decision. He leaned over to me and said, "I'm taking it back down."

I didn't say anything but nodded my head in agreement, thinking, *I hope he can get it back down.*

He did, and told us he'd have the plane looked at again. Without any consultation, the five of us knew we had enough, and I said, "Ken, I think we'll drive back."

We rented a car and even though it took us nearly nine hours to get back home on snow–covered roads we felt very good about being on the ground and taking our time to get back safely.

Word spread quickly about our harrowing experience, helped greatly by Carl Kologie's colorful account in *The Indiana Gazette*. Since Jack Benedict was the one who had arranged the trip, everyone has ever since referred to the flight as "Air Benedict."

And when you go through an experience like that, it forms a bond among the participants. So whenever two or three of us meet at a game or wherever, invariably the subject turns to "Remember the 'Air Benedict' flight to Grand Rapids?"

The one person I hadn't seen for a long time since the flight was the student photographer, Joe Wojcik. A couple of years ago while I was broadcasting a basketball game in Pittsburgh I noticed a man approaching me before the game. He had a camera in hand and was wearing a press credential. He smiled and said "Remember me?"

He looked familiar, but I finally had to admit, "I should know you, but I can't remember where we met."

"Remember the flight to Grand Rapids?" he asked.

Of course then I knew who he was. Smiling, I answered, "How could I ever forget?"

We then relived our brush with extinction.

As I was trying to recall all the facts of this story, I called Jack Benedict to make sure of the details. My final question was, "Jack, do you remember the exact date of the game?"

Without hesitation he replied, "November 18, 1989. I can still see it on my tombstone."

10

ILLEGAL BROADCAST

When I returned to my office at the radio station on Friday afternoon, September 12, 1987, my partner, Mark Harley, was there to greet me. The look on his face told me there was a problem. It didn't take long to find out what the problem was when Harley said, "We can't do the Homer Center game tomorrow afternoon."

"What?" I replied incredulously, "what do you mean we can't do it?"

"The phone company called and said they weren't allowed to install our broadcast line. The man said that when he wanted to know where to install the line, the athletic director at Richland told him we did not have permission to broadcast the game. Apparently we didn't comply with their school board policy, as we had not requested permission to do the game," Harley said.

"Wait a minute I did write to them to request permission," I told Harley.

"Yeah, I know, but their policy says the request must be presented to the school board at least two meetings before the scheduled event, and our request didn't make the deadline."

"That's ridiculous," I fumed. "You mean if I had sent the request a couple of weeks earlier they would have approved it."

"That's what they said," replied Harley.

It didn't take me more than a few seconds to state firmly, "Well, somehow we're going to do that game."

My first move was to call Joe Marcoline, Superintendent of the Homer Center School District. I explained our plight and Joe said he would make a phone call and see what he could do. Twenty minutes later we got our answer. Joe apologized. He said he had done what he could but their school board policy was exactly as we learned earlier and he was told they couldn't deviate from it. Now it was time to get creative.

"Let's see," I said to Harley. "The game is scheduled for one o'clock. Let's move the starting time to 1:45 with the pre game show starting at 1:30. We'll tape the game as it's being played and play the tapes back shortly thereafter."

"How are you going to do that, Ray?" Harley asked.

"Well, Richland High is right next to UPJ, the University of Pittsburgh at Johnstown. We'll go over early tomorrow and find some student in a dorm and pay him to let us use his phone so that we can play the tapes down the phone line." (This of course was long before cell phones or the problem would have been more easily solved.)

So with this plan in mind, Mark Bertig, who was my broadcast partner, and my youngest son, Jason, who was 12 years old, left early Saturday morning for Johnstown. Around 10:30 a. m. we started our search for a phone on the UPJ campus.

MARK BERTIG
I was able to hire him to sell radio advertising and he has gone on to be one of the top executives of Renda Broadcasting. Mark and I are pictured doing a Homer Center basketball game at the Cleveland Cavs old home court in Richfield Coliseum.

When I noticed a couple of boys coming out of a building that looked like a dorm, we walked in to look for a phone. What a mistake! All we saw were girls coming in and out of rooms and one of them asked us, "What do you guys want? This is a girls' dorm."

"Excuse me," I said, as we hurriedly departed the building.

Looking around, we noticed a couple of girls coming from another building to go into the dorm we had just exited. We quickly concluded that this must be a boys' dorm and went inside. We were correct. It didn't take long to find someone to whom we could explain our dilemma and offer to pay for the use of a phone. No problem, we actually had our choice of phones. We selected one, and Jason set up outside in a hallway as the young man who offered his phone not only had such a long phone line that we could extend it beyond his room, but he gave Jason a card table and chair so that we could have our tape recorder ready for playback.

Our plan was beginning to take shape. Next step was to tape the pre-game show which Bertig and I did outside. We gave the tape to Jason and told him to call the radio station collect, give them the number to call back and begin running the pre-game show at 1:30.

Now we knew we had to get the first tape of the first quarter action back to Jason around 1:40 p. m. so he could run it as soon as the pre-game show was over.

Mark and I paid to get into the game, the first and only time I can recall having to do that, because we always sat in the press box and naturally had permission to do the game. We found seats among the Homer Center fans, many of whom we knew, and explained to those immediately around us what we were doing.

The first quarter went fine as I did the play-by-play and Mark provided color commentary. At approximately 1:35, we stopped our first tape and Mark left the game to jump into my car and drive it a short distance to get the tape to Jason in time to run it. Everything went fine because, counting the commercials we were running, we had the timing down pat. Every tape had to be shorter because we had to allow time to run or rather drive them to Jason. So the first tape ran 35 minutes, and the second 30. I drove the second tape to Jason as Mark did second quarter play-by-play.

At halftime we were able to gain some time because we did a short first-half recap and then stopped the tape instead of filling the rest of the half as you would have to do with a live broadcast. Also at halftime, a former Homer Center player sitting next to us offered to drive the second-half tapes to Jason and we gratefully accepted. That way Mark and I could both watch the rest of the game.

It was interesting the way we transferred the rest of the tapes. The young man who volunteered to drive them down would park his car near the fence and when he was ready, we would toss the tape over the fence and he'd be off to get the tape to Jason.

It turned out to be a very good game. It was scoreless nearly the whole way before Richland got a touchdown to win 6-0. With the last tape in hand Mark and I left the game together to get the tape to Jason. I knew we were going to be close on the timing. As we hustled up the steps Jason said "Hurry, Dad. The last commercial is running. Quick, give me the tape."

I popped it out of my recorder and handed it to Jason. He barely got it in the playback unit and didn't have time to cue it when he hit the play button. After what seemed like an eternity of silence, we heard "three, two, one," the countdown cue, and then the play-by-play started. "It was perfect up until now," I said.

As the final tape ran, Mark and I went outside to tape the post-game show, but the pressure was off. We had plenty of time and after Jason played the post-game show we paid the young man whose phone we had used $10, which he was glad to receive, and we were on our way.

Not home, though. You see we had another game, one we were legally permitted to do, at Penns Manor High School in Kenwood, at least an hour away. We grabbed some fast food at a nearby restaurant and, on the trip to Penns Manor, we thoroughly enjoyed reliving the way we outwitted the authorities to air a game we were not permitted to do.

A trip to the confessional would come on Monday.

11

GETTING ON THE AIR

Getting on the air isn't automatic. That's why I always try to be very early when I'm broadcasting a game. You never know what might happen.

I really enjoyed working with Mel Check, who was our engineer for the Duquesne home games for over 20 years. Mel would always be there even before I got there. The equipment was all set up and he would have already contacted the station and have everything set to go. In addition, if any problems developed during the broadcast, Mel invariably would get us right back on the air because he was a trained, experienced engineer.

However, on road games guess who did the engineering? Right, I did. The first couple of years when the Dukes' games were on WJAS, the station would hire engineers on the road and that was great. I just had to show up and it was just like a home game with Mel Check. Everything was set up and ready to go and I could concentrate on calling the game. After all, that's what they were paying me for.

But things change, meaning, in order to save money, it started with me engineering the road games. That meant transporting the equipment, hooking it up, contacting the station, making sure all the commercials ran, etc. Of course I was used to this from having done thousands of games on WDAD in Indiana, Pa. Because we couldn't afford the luxury of having an engineer even on the home games, and I obviously knew something about broadcast equipment; but, and this is a big but, when something went wrong, especially if somehow the equipment failed, I was not and am not an engineer.

But I do understand something about economics. And really, an engineer isn't needed at least 90, maybe 95% of the time. That's because things rarely go wrong, but when they do, well that's the reason for this chapter.

Mel Check was never late for a game, except once. It was a Duquesne game at the Civic Arena on a Saturday afternoon. When I arrived at the arena I noticed Mel wasn't there. I wasn't concerned because it was still an hour and a half before air-time. I thought *well for once I beat Mel to the game.*

But when a half-hour passed and Mel still hadn't shown, I called him. When he answered, I asked him when he was coming to the game. He said, "It's tonight, isn't it?"

"No," I said, "it starts in an hour."

Mel's schedule, obviously one that didn't include a later change, had the game scheduled for Saturday night.

"I'll be there as soon as I can," Mel said.

"Don't worry, Mel, I happen to have the equipment I use on the IUP games in my car. I'll get us going with it."

It didn't take me more than 20 minutes to get my Indiana equipment, hook it up, and get connected with the station.

Just as we were about to go on the air with the pre-game show a man walked up to our broadcast position and identified himself as being with the engineer's union and asked to check my union card.

Well, I had a union card all right, but it was with AFTRA, the union for announcers. I knew immediately I didn't have the identification the man was seeking. I hesitated momentarily and fate stepped in. The man said, "Oh, I recognize you. You're okay."

He may have recognized me but not as an engineer for the Duquesne broadcasts. Anyhow, I didn't correct him, and we went on the air with my Indiana equipment.

Mel arrived shortly thereafter and was able to set up his equipment and during a commercial made the switch. Disaster averted.

———

I recall an IUP basketball game against Edinboro in Edinboro. On the IUP games we traveled with the team by bus on road games and arrived in plenty of time to hook up our equipment. The only problem this time was that the line didn't check out. In those ancient days, we had one-way feeds. Now it's different, and much better. So we would hook up our equipment, make a phone call, and tell the operator at WDAD to listen on cue to see whether he was hearing us. In this case, nothing. We tried different terminals on the block and still nothing.

I then called the telephone company and by the time they ran a check we were now only 45 minutes before air-time. I was told they would dispatch a technician as soon as possible, but, as he was coming from Erie, it would take 25 or 30 minutes.

We waited anxiously and by the time the technician arrived Edinboro's gym was packed. In fact they were using closed-circuit TV into another building on campus because they knew they would have an overflow crowd.

As soon as we met the technician and showed him where we were hooking up, he said, "No wonder you have a problem. Didn't anyone tell you we moved the line across the floor? I guess no one took out the old line. You were hooking up to a dead line."

Great, I thought, as I looked at wall-to-wall people across the floor and noted that the technician had said we were right in the middle of the bleachers. *How were we going to squeeze in there among all those Edinboro fans?*

But that's when the technician "took the bull by the horns."

"Grab your equipment and follow me," he said.

The three of us walked right across the middle of the floor while the teams were warming up on either end.

"Excuse me," he said four or five times as he plowed through Edinboro students en route to the fifth row of bleachers. As we dutifully followed him we heard more than a couple of unprintable comments.

The technician located the line, helped us set up our equipment and with his portable phone checked out the line to make sure we were getting through to the station. We tried to be as friendly as possible to the fans around us as we literally were shoe-horned in among them. We had the equipment sandwiched between our feet and our scorebooks on our laps.

To say the technician was terrific is an understatement. He went over and above the call of duty.

The game itself was a thriller. With Edinboro leading by one point and ten seconds to go Dick Crawford hit a jump shot for IUP to give them a one-point lead. Edinboro moved the ball up the floor and with two seconds to go hit a miracle shot that gave them a one-point lead. The fans were on their feet shouting and getting ready to celebrate the Edinboro victory. We had to get up too to view the action on the floor. But hold everything. The trailing official was blowing his whistle. He was ruling that because Edinboro had called a time-out before the shot went in the shot didn't count. The timer put two more seconds on the clock and of course the fans became irate at the ruling.

After the time-out IUP played good defense and Edinboro's last-second desperation shot missed, giving the Indians the thrilling victory.

Naturally I was excited describing the action; but the student fans who surrounded us and just moments ago had been celebrating, all of a sudden became deadly silent in disappointment. Then when they heard me enthusiastically describing the IUP win they all turned in unison and started booing me and pointing their fingers at me, and for a moment it looked as though I was going to be attacked. I wisely toned down my excitement and somehow the moment passed without real trouble.

All the events surrounding the question of whether we would get on the air at all, and then to be seated right in the midst of the Edinboro students, together with the thrilling, controversial end of the game made the experience one for the ages.

There have been many other hair-raising close calls getting games on the air, including a Junior Legion baseball play-off game in Pottstown, Pa., when we had to tap into a phone at the Pottstown High School. We had to connect to the block where the phone lines came into the school, which happened to be in the school's boiler room. I remember searching around in the dark for the telephone terminals, hooking up the line, and then running over 600 feet of line before we simply ran out of phone line. Fortunately that took us down the left-field line near third base, an excellent vantage point from which to call the game.

The problem was that when you run that much line you have a couple of places where you have to splice it to another line. I think we had three places where we did this and more than once fans who were coming to the game would inadvertently kick the wire and twice the splices came apart, meaning we were off the air immediately. We would quickly re-splice the wire and re-dial and get on the air once again.

Another game at Alliance College in Cambridge Springs, Pa., challenged our creativity. For some reason there had been no phone line installed for our broadcast. I don't know who goofed but there we were with no way to broadcast until I spotted a pay phone not far from one of the entrances to the floor. So we used the pay phone by taking off the mouthpiece and alligator clipping our phone line to the two leads and running line to the one entrance-way to the gym. We set up a table and were able to call the game from there even though one corner to our right was totally obscured from our view. Hey, you do what you have to do to get the game on the air.

Perhaps the most humorous situation in getting a game on the air occurred in Boyertown, Pa. Boyertown always had excellent Junior Legion baseball teams and would invariably win the state championship, and most years would host the annual state tournament.

Indiana County also had an excellent Junior Legion baseball program and virtually every year would qualify at least one, and usually two, and sometimes three teams for the state tournament. We would attempt to do every game possible featuring the local teams at the state tournament. This required some incredible planning and switching from one game to another if two were played simultaneously and one game was more exciting than the other.

Because of some rain outs on the first day of the 1986 state tournament in Boyertown, one of the teams we were following, after losing their first game in the double elimination tourney, was suddenly assigned to a field that wasn't on the original schedule. What this meant was we didn't have a phone line installed there. When we told the tournament officials about our dilemma, they said we could use the phone from the Gablesville Athletic Club, which was across the road from the field.

My broadcast partner, Mark Bertig, and I hustled over to Gablesville, knowing we had less than an hour to get set up to do the next game. And that's where the fun started.

We arrived at the field to discover that we would have to run about 250 feet of phone line to get from the phone behind the bar at the Athletic Club to the field, and we had somehow to get it across a road that ran alongside the field.

First off, the bartender at the Legion wasn't the most accommodating person. He reluctantly pointed out where the phone was and when we told him that once the game started he could no longer use the phone until the game was over, he was not pleased.

Getting across the road was another obstacle. We just couldn't run the line on the road because cars driving up and down would obviously tear it up and that would be the end of the broadcast. We were able to borrow a ladder and climb up a telephone pole on one side of the road and suspend the line over the road to our broadcast position. One of the locals pointed out that this would not work because trucks also used this road and the line wasn't high enough to clear a truck.

We noticed that there was a shed along the right field line and figured if we could get the line from the pole to the shed it would be high enough. Then it would be easy to run the line from the shed to our broadcast position near the backstop to the right of home plate.

Jim Kundla, a good friend who was attending the tournament along with Buddy Jones, volunteered to climb the ladder and get on the shed where he would somehow secure our line. Jim was able to accomplish this but not before he cut his hand badly on a piece of jagged tin. After the game Mark accompanied Jim to the hospital where they had to wait five hours before Jim's hand was treated.

Once we were all hooked up, I called the station collect, as I recall, to tell my son David, who was working the board, that we were just about set up to go. I gave David the number to call back and told him to wait five minutes then call us.

About five minutes later the phone rang and I hurriedly grabbed it and said, "Hello," fully expecting to hear David's voice.

Instead I heard a woman say, "Is my husband John there?"

Oh, oh, I thought, *some lady is looking for her husband and I don't have time to run back to the bar and try to find him, and then let him get on the phone with his wife. We're ready to go on the air.*

After just a moment's hesitation, I said, "Sorry ma'am, John isn't here," and I hung up.

When I told Mark Bertig what happened, he just burst into laughter. The phone then rang again and this time it was my son David and we were all set to broadcast the game.

I've often wondered what happened when John returned home that day to face the certain wrath of his wife. Hopefully it didn't end in divorce court.

12

THE NBA, ALMOST

In 1978 CBS telecast NBA basketball games using a regional concept. The thinking was that people in the East, for example, would rather see the Knicks and the Celtics; in the Midwest, the Bulls versus the Pistons, etc.

I became aware, through Beano Cook who was working in publicity at CBS in New York, that CBS might be looking for additional talent. Beano was a Pittsburgher and longtime Sports Information Director at the University of Pittsburgh where I got to know him because Duquesne played Pitt every year. When I contacted Beano about the NBA he used his influence to help set up an audition for me.

And to CBS TV's credit they know how to do an audition. I was assigned to do the play-by-play of a game between the Indiana Pacers and the Los Angeles Lakers in Indianapolis on January 8, 1978.

While the game would be broadcast live on CBS TV with Don Criqui doing the play-by-play, my version of the game would be video taped for CBS to evaluate.

I was informed that Gene Shue and Herb Brown, two former coaches, would also be auditioning by doing the color commentary, one half each.

CBS sent me my airline ticket and said they'd pay me $500 to do the audition tape, plus expenses.

The flight was scheduled to leave Pittsburgh Saturday afternoon for the Sunday afternoon game. When Gene Shue contacted me, we arranged to meet for dinner at the Hyatt in Indianapolis, where we would be staying. I was thrilled because Gene Shue was someone I had been aware of since he starred in college at Maryland, played pro ball and coached in the pros. Besides, I had heard he was a pretty good tennis player, which would give us another connection, since I also play tennis.

As I was waiting for my flight in Pittsburgh, a flight from Philadelphia arrived and I discovered that this was the plane that would be going to Indianapolis. Then, to my amazement, as the passengers deplaned, several members of the Lakers appeared. There was Coach Jerry West, players Adrian Dantley, Keith Wilkes, and Kareem Abdul-Jabbar. I began looking for Norm Nixon. Finally he walked off the plane. He smiled broadly when he spotted me.

Nixon had played and starred at Duquesne from 1973-1977 and was a first-round draft pick of the Lakers. Since I had broadcast all of his college games, naturally I got to know him.

After the "What are you doing here, Ray?" Norm and I chatted about how his rookie season with the Lakers was going.

Nixon introduced me to some of the Laker players who were nearby, including Pat Riley, who was doing the "color" on the Lakers radio broadcasts. It was then that we found out our flight to Indianapolis had been delayed because of a snowstorm in the Midwest.

Riley, in addition to his radio chores, also served as the travel coordinator for the Lakers when they were on the road. And he immediately said to me, "Ray, why don't you give me your ticket and I'll include it with those of our group. That way it will make it easier for you, especially if we have to get another flight." I thanked him and after a delay of an hour and a half we were on our way to Indy.

I met Gene Shue for dinner and we talked about the upcoming game briefly, but mostly we talked tennis, since we were both avid players.

Then came the game. Don Criqui was seated not 15 feet to my right doing the live telecast. We had our own producer for the video taped version. Gene Shue did the color the first half and Herb Brown the second. When the game ended I took off my headset mike and thought *Well I'm satisfied with the job I did. Now it's up to CBS.*

The following week I got a call from the woman (I forget her name) who was my contact at CBS. "Well, there's no question you know how to do play-by-play," she said.

"Here's what's next. We'll send you a contract that calls for you to be paid $1500 a game with a guarantee that you'll be paid for at least three games. In other words if you do just one game, and it doesn't work out, we still have to pay you for three games."

That sounded good to me.

She went on, "We'll probably assign you to a game involving New Orleans and Houston, for example, because there would be three or four stations involved and we'd get the chance to see how you do in a smaller region."

Then she continued, "Of course there are no guarantees. What I'm outlining is possible if we expand the idea of doing more regional telecasts next season."

I was on Cloud Nine, and already couldn't wait until the next NBA season. A few days later a complicated contract from CBS arrived in the mail, $1500 a game, a guarantee of payment for three games even if I did only one, plus all expenses. Of course it was all contingent on my being hired to do at least one game.

That year, Portland met Philadelphia in the NBA finals, with the Blazers winning the title.

Portland was one of the smallest markets in the NBA. Philly was bigger but couldn't compare to New York, L. A., or Chicago. The result—very low ratings for the NBA finals. The CBS bigwigs then decided to scrap the regional telecasts completely and go with an NBA Game of the Week. That meant they needed only one play–by–play announcer and Brent Musburger was that person.

I still have the unexecuted contract.

The NBA, almost.

13

COUSY AND SHARMAN

I remember watching NBA basketball on TV in the late '50s and '60s when Bob Cousy and Bill Sharman were the backcourt wonders of the Boston Celtics.

Cousy was the point guard who piloted the Celtics' fast-break, and even if he wasn't the first basketball player to dribble behind his back (I understand Bob Davies was really the first.), Cooz was the one who popularized the maneuver that is mainstream at all levels of basketball today.

Sharman was the sharp shooting guard who seemingly never missed when Cousy got him the ball. His shooting style was flawless, elbow straight down, ball cradled loosely resting on the finger tips of his right hand, and with the flip of the wrist, invariably the ball swished through the basket or glanced off the backboard at precisely the right angle to nestle in the net.

I marveled at these two magicians of the backcourt and when I began my broadcasting career in Indiana, Pa., as the morning deejay and sports announcer, I was thrilled when one day in 1960 Joe Termin,

the manager of radio station WDAD, asked me whether I would like to accompany him to Punxsutawney to see and hear Bob Cousy, who would be the featured speaker at a banquet there.

KEN WILLIAMS, BOB COUSY,
JOE TERMIN, AND YOURS TRULY
Ken was the highly successful basketball coach at Marion Center High School. Bob Cousy I think you know about. Joe Termin was the General Manager of WDAD in Indiana, PA, who hired me in November, 1958, and was always a great friend

Joe said, "You might want to bring your tape recorder

because they're having a get-together with the press beforehand and you might get a chance to interview Cousy."

Wow, that would be something, I thought. So I grabbed my Wollensak tape recorder. This was 1960, long before cassette or digital recorders. The Wollensak was a bulky reel-to-reel machine that needed AC power to operate, but it worked fine once it was set up.

Joe and I motored the half-hour to Punxsutawney from Indiana and all I could think about was whether I would be able to get a personal interview with Bob Cousy and if I did, what would I ask him.

We arrived in time to join some other media people and dignitaries in a room near the main banquet hall. Cousy was dressed in a blue blazer with white shirt and red striped tie and already had a circle of people around him. After a bit, he wandered away from the group and I hustled over, introduced myself, and asked him whether he would give me a few minutes to tape an interview. Without hesitating, he agreed and I nervously but quickly set up my Wollensak and tape-recorded the interview. But that's not what this story is all about.

At the banquet later, when the meal was finished, and Bob Cousy had spoken for perhaps 20 or 25 minutes, he then said, "We have a few more minutes, does anyone have a question?"

Well there must have been 300 people in that banquet hall and no one raised his or her hand. After what seemed like an embarrassing eternity, it became obvious to me that everyone was too stagestruck to ask the great Bob Cousy a question. Even though I had my interview on tape, I felt I had to save the day by asking at least one question, so I raised my hand. I was sitting about midway back in the audience when Cousy spotted my raised hand. He pointed at me and said, "Ray."

I was flabbergasted. Cousy actually remembered my name. Yes, I had met him and interviewed him about two hours ago and I remembered how thrilled I was that when as he answered my questions in the interview, he called me by name several times. But he had met and shaken the hands of hundreds of people the past couple of hours and here he was picking me out of the crowd and saying "Ray" as if we were bosom buddies.

To say I was greatly impressed is a gross understatement.

Fast forward now 43 years to December, 2003. I'm still broadcasting sporting events and on this night I have my cassette tape recorder set up at the Apollo Ridge High School gym for a girls' basketball game. I am going to tape record the varsity game for rebroadcast the next day on WTYM in Kittanning, Pa.

From a small table they had provided me, set up at mid-court across from the scorer's table, I was watching the second half of the girls' JV game. At one point a group of people passed in front of me and sat in the bleachers to my left. In the group there was a gentleman who caught my attention. My immediate thought was *that sure looks like Bill Sharman.*

I watched as the four people in the group climbed the bleachers to take seats near the top row. I couldn't take my eyes off the one man though. I had never seen Bill Sharman in person. My recollections of him were from the

BILL SHARMAN
Sharpshooting All–Star guard for the Boston Celtics in the '50s and '60s and teammate of Bob Cousy. Elected to Basketball Hall of Fame both as a player and a coach.

TV screen when I watched him play for the Celtics in the '50s and '60s. And of course I had seen his picture in various sports magazines through the years, but none recently. Yet, if I could erase 30 years or so from the man I'm looking at in the bleachers, it sure looks like Bill Sharman, or, at worst, his brother.

Entering into my thinking was the fact that I knew Bill Sharman and his wife had recently bought a house in Indiana, Pa. I knew this because Chuck Klausing, the former football coach at Indiana University of Pennsylavania, had told me. Chuck said that Bill's wife was from the area originally and that they had bought a house on North 6th Street in Indiana. And others had told me of Bill Sharman sightings on the streets of downtown Indiana.

But I was at Apollo Ridge and even though it's only about 20 miles from Indiana, I began thinking, *what in the world would Bill Sharman be doing here watching a girls' high school basketball game?*

What should I do? I have enough time before the varsity game to go into the stands and either make a fool of myself if it turns out he isn't Bill Sharman or verify my original suspicion that this is indeed the famous basketball Hall of Famer.

Just as I was summoning the courage to go into the bleachers, lo and behold, all four members of the "Sharman" party came down from the bleachers, and one of the men said to me, "Ray, I want you to meet someone."

The man who spoke was Mike McLay, whom I immediately recognized. You see I was concentrating my attention so much on the man I thought was Bill Sharman that I hadn't even looked at the people who accompanied him.

As soon as Mike McLay said "I want you to meet someone," I knew it had to be Bill Sharman. I lit up like a Christmas tree and said, "You don't have to tell me who this is" as I happily greeted Bill Sharman.

As we chatted I quickly found out that Mike was Bill's brother-in-law and that Bill was at the game to watch his niece, Mike's daughter Katie, play for the Apollo Ridge girls' team.

When I met Bill Sharman, I was 66 years old, but I'm sure I must have gushed as I did when I met his backcourt mate Bill Cousy 43 years ago when I was a young pup of 23. Naturally I had to tell Sharman my Cousy story and how pleased I was now to meet him. He was very gracious and we chatted for several minutes prior to the girls' varsity game.

After the PA announcer gave the starting line ups for the varsity game, he then told the crowd that there was a special guest in the audience that night. Then he introduced Bill Sharman, who rose and waved to the appreciative fans.

But there's more to this story too, just as there was for the Cousy story.

I went on to describe the action of the first half of the Apollo Ridge girls' game. At halftime I did a brief recap, then turned off my tape recorder to await the start of the second half.

Shortly after the second half began, fans were still coming back from the concession stands and rest rooms and naturally they passed right in front of me sitting at mid-court. I had to get up quickly to see around the fans in order to continue describing the action. Then a lone gentleman started to pass in front of me. It was Bill Sharman returning to his seat. I got ready to get on my feet again to get a clear view of the floor when Bill suddenly stooped over as low as he could get and hustled past my broadcast position.

I was dumbfounded. Here was Bill Sharman, still rather nimble for a man in his mid-70's, and he was so aware of what I was doing that he wanted to make sure he didn't obstruct my view. Maybe it's not a big thing, but I was impressed all the more about what kind of person Bill Sharman is.

Cousy and Sharman, two great basketball players, who affected first a young and then veteran sports announcer by their very gracious behavior and good manners.

14

RACIST?

Many times I've thought that if I were just paid a penny for every word I have uttered the past 50 years doing play-by-play I'd be a rich man.

And when you say millions of words occasionally a few of them can get you into trouble.

Joe Termin and I were driving to Slippery Rock in 1960 to broadcast the Indiana State College-Slippery Rock basketball game. And we were discussing what strategy Indiana should employ if they hoped to win. It's called second guessing if you do it after the fact; so I was trying to exhibit my vast basketball expertise by offering my prediction and what we, Indiana, should be doing to win the game.

"Joe," I said, "Indiana should use a zone the whole game because I don't think they can match up man-to-man with Slippery Rock. And you know what, they won't do it because they're committed to man-to-man and only use a zone as a last resort."

I can't remember whether Joe agreed with me or not, but I continued. "And if they play man they're going to fall behind right away and have trouble catching up because the fans will be pumped up and Slippery Rock will have all the momentum they need."

Our broadcast location at Slippery Rock in Morrow Field House was far from the best. It was in the last row of the bleachers and we had to position our broadcast equipment by our feet and balance our scorebooks on our laps.

As the game started, Indiana played man-to-man and Slippery Rock jumped out to an 11 to 2 lead in the first three minutes before Indiana called a timeout, hopefully to go to a zone I thought.

I called for a 60-second commercial from the station, lowered my hand-held mike, looked at Joe and said, "What the hell are we doing playing man-to-man?"

Back then the broadcast lines we had installed for road games only permitted us a one-way feed. In other words we could transmit but had no feedback from the station. So once we hooked up we'd go to a pay phone and check to make sure the station was receiving us. From then on everything was by cue. The radio station operator listened to us and we did a countdown when we wanted to go on the air and when we called for a commercial we timed the break and returned when the ad was over.

When the operator at the station was "on the ball," which was most of the time, everything would go smoothly. Once in a while, though, the operator might miss a cue and of course whatever was said during the break would go over the air, unknown to the broadcasters.

Guess what happened when I made my critical comment about Indiana's defense? Right, it went on the air. Fortunately my mike was lowered and with the crowd whooping it up because Slippery Rock had started so quickly, it was somewhat muffled, or so I was later told.

I didn't know any of this until the next day when more than one person said something to me along the lines of "did you say 'what the hell'?" Sheepishly I had to admit that I had.

Nothing further resulted from the incident, thankfully. But I learned a lesson that day that every broadcaster should know: always assume that your mike is "live," even if it's not supposed to be.

————————————————————

But this chapter is entitled "Racist?" and here's that story.

It was time for IUP's Christmas Tree Festival Tournament, held annually between Christmas and New Year's. It was a two-day event with doubleheaders both nights and IUP was the host team.

The night before the tourney, IUP Coach Herm Sledzik hosted a party at his home with the coaches from all four teams, media, and other dignitaries in attendance.

Since our radio station WDAD would be broadcasting the Indiana games it was a good way to meet the other coaches and get background information on their teams.

Indiana played the second game on the first night. The first game was won by Maryland State, who employed a fast-breaking style of ball. After the game I congratulated their coach, whom I had met the night before and asked him if he would join us at halftime of the Indiana game for an interview. He readily agreed.

Indiana had a big lead at the half of their game and it certainly looked like it would be Indiana versus Maryland State the next night for the championship.

I began my interview by congratulating Maryland State's Coach on his team's victory, and then I said to him, "Coach, you're watching Indiana play a very deliberate style of game, at times taking up to a minute before attempting a shot. Your team, on the other hand, plays run-and-gun basketball, many times taking the first shot available. How do you think your style will match up with Indiana's if they go on and win?"

He replied, "First of all I resent the fact that you call our style "run-and-gun basketball. Just because we're a black school you obviously think we don't have the discipline to play like Indiana. This is just how we play and it's not run-and-gun, it's called pro-style offense."

HERM SLEDZIK
Former Penn State basketball star, then successful head coach and finally athletic director at IUP. Tagged with the nickname "Legs" in high school. A great guy with a winning personality.

I couldn't believe he said what he did, but I knew he said it because I was hearing it in my headset. Fortunately I reacted quickly enough to reply, "Coach, I think it's just a question of semantics, I call it run-and-gun, you call it pro-style offense, but believe me, I certainly didn't mean to disparage your team, which plays an exciting brand of ball."

I then went on quickly to ask another question so that we didn't get hung up in a debate, and amazingly the rest of the interview went on without further incident.

The next day I got more than a couple of comments about the halftime interview, and I learned my lesson. Never again have I referred to a fast paced game as being "run-and-gun" basketball.

15

SNOWSTORM

On November 11, 1994 I found myself in Hartford, Connecticut, scheduled to broadcast my first game of the Continental Basketball season between the Pittsburgh Piranhas and the Hartford Hellcats.

At halftime, I interviewed Vince Cazzetta, a scout for the Toronto Raptors, who would enter the NBA in 1985.

Vince was semi-retired after coaching in the college and pro ranks, most notably at Seattle University and as coach of the champion Pittsburgh Pipers of the then 1968 brand new American Basketball Association. You

VINCE CAZZETTA
Longtime successful basketball coach who piloted the Pittsburgh Pipers to the first ever ABA Basketball Championship in 1968.

remember the league, the one that featured the red, white, and blue basketball.

Since this was Pittsburgh's first foray back into the pro ranks with the Piranhas, naturally we talked about his success with the Pipers in '68. The interview went well and when we went to commercial I thanked Vince and suggested we exchange business cards. Selfishly, in the back of my mind I felt Vince could be a valuable contact as far as my aspirations to do NBA broadcasts were concerned. Besides I felt we genuinely "hit if off" and I sensed Vince was the kind of person you would enjoy calling a friend.

And the friendship did develop over the years, mainly with occasional phone calls to talk basketball. Then in 1996 Vince told me about his desire to produce a video of "The Championship Season" when he coached the Piranhas to the first ever ABA title. He told me he had secured the rights to the video tapes of the seven-game championship series between the Pipers and the New Orleans Buccaneers. Besides, as he informed me, he had a large scrapbook of articles and photos covering the Pittsburgh team throughout the season.

Most importantly, as I would find out later, Vince had an excellent memory and a vivid way of describing many of the unusual events of that most memorable season. And Vince wanted me to narrate the video including interviewing him on camera, and literally produce the whole undertaking.

After I had viewed the videos and scripted as much as I could, Vince contacted a production firm in Connecticut to arrange studio time to shoot the video. He was underwriting the whole production with the expectation that there would be so many basketball fans who would buy the video that he wouldn't "lose his shirt." And even if he did, he wanted to do it so there would be a visual record of that history-making season.

Now here's where things get interesting. If we had shot the video without a hitch, this chapter would never have made it into the book.

On April 1, 1996, I began driving to Vince's home in Simsbury, Connecticut. We had planned to work that day on the format so that we wouldn't waste too much valuable studio time the next day. Vince also insisted I stay at his home.

As I headed out of Indiana, Pa. up to interstate 80 I was aware they were calling for a snowstorm, but I figured, *How bad could it be in April?* Well, it began snowing about two hours into my proposed seven-hour drive and when I headed north on route 81 toward Scranton the snow was so extremely heavy that the travel was becoming treacherous.

Reporters on radio stations in the area were telling people to stay off the roads. But what could I do? I continued, and when I headed down a hill and had to touch the brakes I lost complete control of my car. As I spun, my car whacked into an SUV on my right and now I was completely turned around going backward and trying desperately to get control of my car. Worse yet, there was a Ryder truck right behind me, with the driver staring me right in the face. I was trying to slow down and so was he. Amazingly, my car then did another 180-degree turn so that I was now going in the right direction and I ended up on the shoulder and was able to get my car to stop without any further damage. The Ryder truck veered around me and pulled off on the right a couple of hundred feet ahead of me. The SUV that I had collided with was nowhere in sight.

The driver of the truck came over my way to see whether I was okay. I informed him that outside of being a little shaken, I was fine. I asked him, "How did you know to go to the left to avoid hitting me?"

He said, "I don't know. I saw your car was out of control and I just guessed 'go left' and it turned out to be the right move."

After I thanked him for checking on me and guessing "right," I mean left, I checked the rear end area of my car which had struck the SUV. There was some damage, but it wasn't bad. I began wondering how much damage the SUV had sustained, hoping it was negligible because it was a heavier vehicle than my Ford Probe.

I got into my car and started out slowly again on the slick and snow- covered I-81 still thinking about the SUV. Not a half-mile down the road I saw the SUV pulled off to the right and the driver checking the damage to the right rear side of his vehicle.

I pulled off behind him, went up to him, introduced myself, and said "I was the one who hit your car."

He was surprised and thanked me for stopping and we exchanged information while I assured him it was totally my fault and I would report that to my insurance company. While we were talking I noticed that there was a woman with a child in the SUV and naturally I assumed it was his wife and child. We shook hands. He thanked me again, and it was back to driving in the snowstorm.

As you might imagine, the going was very slow. The snow was still pelting down and there were fewer cars on the road when I turned onto route 84, which would take me across New York state into Connecticut.

After another hour of going at most 20 miles an hour, I found the interstate was now reduced to one lane, with cars pulled off to both sides of the road everywhere. My windshield wipers were caked with ice and I was having difficulty seeing, but I didn't want to stop for fear of never being able to get going again. Then the car in front of me came to a dead stop and I had to stop.

I had no idea where I was exactly but I knew I couldn't continue. I got out of my car and walked up to the car in front of me. The driver rolled down his window when he saw me, and I asked him whether he knew of any lodging nearby. He said, "There's a motel at the next exit about a half-mile up the road if we ever get going again." I thanked him, went back to my car, cleared the ice from my wipers, and got back in. Eventually the traffic ahead started to move again, although now it was at a rate between five and ten miles an hour. I thought if I can only get to the exit and find that motel.

After about ten minutes I thought I perceived an exit to the right, but the sign was so completely snow-covered that I really couldn't tell whether there was a road or not. But I took a chance and headed right, into even deeper snow, speeding up a bit so that I wouldn't get stuck. Ahead of me I could barely make out a couple of buildings, but I could see cars parked every which way next to both buildings. Just as I edged off the road, my car came to a complete stop in a snowdrift.

I got out to find the snow up to my thighs. I noticed I was parked near a restaurant and up the hill there was a motel. I started trudging through the thigh-high snow and when I entered the motel all I could see were people everywhere. They were packed in front of the check-in desk, they were sitting on every available chair and couch in the lobby, and others were simply lying on the floor. *Good luck in getting a room I thought.*

I waited patiently and finally talked to the clerk to affirm the inevitable. There simply was no more room. But I was welcome to search for space somewhere on a chair or on the floor.

I noticed the typical motel bar just off the lobby was also teeming with mankind. But I squirmed in and found that even though they didn't serve food they had cheese and crackers and chips set out. When I discovered one chair at a table already accommodating seven other people I asked if they wouldn't mind if I joined them.

"No problem," several of them said in unison.

After I introduced myself, the war stories began, or rather continued. And it turned out that among the group was a couple from Butler, Pa., not far from Indiana, Pa. Naturally we started comparing notes about whom we knew from each area. It turned out that they knew more people from my area than I did theirs, but there was at least one person I actually knew that they knew. Now get this, after a few more minutes of conversation and cheese and crackers and both soft and hard drinks, depending on the individual, I found out that the couple from Butler had been here a couple of hours and had actually secured a room. And when they found out I didn't have one they offered to let me stay in their room. The man even went to the desk and found they could put a roll-a-way bed in the room. I protested, but not too strongly, and reluctantly agreed, while insisting I would pay my share.

But they would have none of it. The only thing I was able to do was give the man my winter coat, because he had left his in his car which was parked in a snowdrift 100 yards or so from the motel. He said he and his wife wanted to get more to eat than cheese and crackers. Naturally they invited me to join them. But I declined, saying that I somehow had to get through to my wife and Vince and let them know what was going on. That's when I offered the man my coat and he agreed to take it rather than to trudge through the snow to get his.

When they left for dinner I headed for the two pay phones off the lobby. The lines were both at least ten deep. Just then I noticed a girl with a room key in her hand heading to what I supposed was her room. I inquired whether it would be possible to use her phone since I needed to call two people and it was important I do that as soon as possible. Without hesitation she said, "Okay, follow me." Talk about being trustworthy.

I used her phone and my credit card to report to Dee and Vince all that had happened. Both of course were concerned, but I assured them that I was all right and that I would stay the night at the motel thanks to the generosity of the couple from Butler. Vince also told me that he and most of Connecticut had been without power most of the day and that there was no way we would be able to shoot the video the next day anyhow. We agreed to reschedule.

After making the phone calls I returned to the lobby, where I saw the man whose SUV I had hit. He smiled. We shook hands and he introduced me to his wife and youngster. His wife said, "I can't believe you stopped, because there was no way we knew who hit us."

I replied I was glad they had pulled over because I didn't know whether I would ever find out whom I had hit. Of course they were stuck too and without a room but happy to be safely under cover.

This story is nearly over. There is but one more notable item. When the couple from Butler came back, I joined them in their room. During our conversation they found out that I broadcast basketball etc., and although I could tell that neither of them was a sports fan, I learned that they knew that the NCAA championship game between Kentucky and Syracuse was on that night; and I was delighted when they asked me if I wanted to watch it. Can you imagine that? I protested, saying I knew they weren't basketball fans, but they said there was really nothing else on they wanted to watch and they would watch it with me. And they did. I made sure I got their names and addresses and promised to write to them when I got back home to thank them, which I did. My only regret is that though I've searched high and low I simply cannot find their names and so can't include them in this story.

The next morning we woke to the sun shining and the snow melting. I again profusely thanked my roommates, dug my car out of the snowdrift in which it was buried, and drove without incident back home to Indiana, Pa.

Vince had re-scheduled our studio time for two weeks later and without further incident we shot "The First ABA Championship."

Vince Cazzetta died in 2005 at the age of 79.

I miss him and I'll never forget him.

16

FORBIDDEN FRUIT

Mike Rice coached the basketball team at Duquesne from 1978 until 1983. And, like all coaches, Mike had his idiosyncrasies. One of these regularly appeared when the Dukes went on the road, for we always rented station wagons rather than have a bus transport us from the airport to the hotel to the game site.

We would normally have four station wagons. Assistant Coach Bruce Bauer would drive one, Trainer Bob Milie another, Sports Information Director Nellie King a third, and I would drive the fourth wagon. We did everything we could to keep Mike from getting behind the wheel, because he drove just as he coached, aggressively.

Mike developed his reputation for being aggressive when he played at Duquesne in 1961 and '62. He was a tenacious defender and seemed to spend as much time on the floor diving for loose balls as he did running or dribbling.

One time, having deliberately gone to the floor, he just managed to slide to the sideline where the opponent's pep band was stationed. The percussion section featured a bass drum that obviously Rice didn't "cotton" to. And Mike, as he came to his feet right next to the drum, "accidentally" put his foot right through the middle of the drum, which greatly reduced its effectiveness.

As a head coach, Mike would do "whatever it takes" to win. At home games at the Civic Arena, he more than once just happened to have at the foul line a better free throw shooter than the Duquesne player who had actually been fouled.

Of course he would deny it. Rice was able to do this back in the late '70s and early '80s when home teams usually had officials who were assigned by the local chapters. I'm not saying they would "look the other way" when Rice attempted to make sure the "right" man was on the line for Duquesne, but he was still able to accomplish it more than once. In fact, WTAE Television in Pittsburgh was able to document it by shooting films and sharing their discovery with their audience. Rice with his effervescent personality, would simply laugh it off.

In 1979, we had a two-game road trip to Florida. We were to play Stetson College in Deland on a Thursday, and were scheduled to play Jacksonville on Saturday. We lost to Stetson by nine and the next day we boarded our station wagons for the trip to Jacksonville.

Before leaving Deland, Mike informed us that Glenn Wilkes, the Stetson coach, had graciously arranged for us to stop at an orange grove en route so that we could each pick a bag of oranges and grapefruit. Everyone in the traveling party was provided a mesh bag for the fruit he would pick.

Mike hopped into the lead car, driven by Bruce Bauer, and said, "Follow me. I have the directions to the orange grove."

So our caravan of four station wagons proceeded toward Jacksonville. Some twenty minutes along the way the lead wagon pulled off the highway with the three remaining wagons following suit.

Pointing to a beautiful grove of trees adorned with the orange fruit, Mike directed, "There it is, guys. Don't waste any time. Fill up your bags and let's get on our way."

We had been picking the fruit for only five minutes when a Florida State Police car pulled up behind our station wagons and two uniformed policemen walked into the grove. The first officer asked, "Who's in charge here?" Instinctively everyone pointed to Coach Rice.

The officer approached Mike, "What's going on here?"

Mike explained that we were the Duquesne basketball team and that Coach Glenn Wilkes of the Stetson team had arranged for us to pick some fruit at this orange grove. The officer said, "Well, that will be easy

MIKE RICE
One of the most colorful coaches in Duquesne basketball history, and longtime "color" commentator for the Portland Trailblazers. Number 44 is Duquesne's Bruce Atkins.

74

enough to check. I'll just call Coach Wilkes to verify your story."

While Mike was busy with the one officer, the players engaged the other officer in conversation, and one of them had the bright idea of asking the officer if he wouldn't mind handcuffing one of his teammates so that he could take a picture. The officer politely declined, having difficulty suppressing his amusement. After all, this was a serious matter.

The other officer meanwhile was having a good bit of trouble getting in touch with Coach Wilkes. It seems he was out and it wasn't clear when he would return. The officer then told Coach Rice, "I know who owns this grove. I'll call him. He'll surely be able to straighten this out."

Unfortunately for Coach Rice and his team, the owner declared he had no knowledge of any arrangement for the Duquesne basketball players to pick oranges from his grove. He did allow, however, that perhaps his son had made the arrangements. He advised that his son should be back "soon."

Well, "soon" turned into a half-hour, then forty-five minutes, and the team had practice time scheduled at Jacksonville. That's when Mike Rice showed his leadership and salesmanship ability. He convinced the officers that there was no way his team would be so blatant as to just pull off the road and start picking oranges illegally. After all, Duquesne was a Catholic University and he wouldn't risk the bad publicity, let alone the possible loss of his job over a few oranges.

The officers finally relented, but they took the necessary information from Mike's driver's license and noted where we were staying in Jacksonville. We tossed our bags of oranges and grapefruit into the wagons and set out for Jacksonville.

Later we found out from the Florida State Police that indeed they had verified that we had permission to pick oranges, but not from the grove at which we had picked them!

It seems Mike had us stop at the wrong grove. Fortunately the owner of the grove where we picked the fruit declined to press charges and there were no further repercussions.

A story like this doesn't die easily though. I devoted my complete pre-game show prior to the broadcast of the Jacksonville game to the orange caper, and Russ Franke, who covered the Dukes for the *Pittsburgh Press* also filed a story, which hit the national news wire and popped up in newspapers throughout the country.

I remember that when we finally got to Jacksonville and had checked into our hotel, I couldn't wait to taste one of those juicy oranges. And was it ever good! I had to eat it standing over the sink because the juice was actually running down my arms and dripping off my elbows into the sink.

I smiled as I thought, *forbidden fruit never tasted so good.*

17

LISTENING TO THE LISTENERS

I've had people ask me over the years "How did you learn how to do play-by-play?"

Well, I learned by listening.

My earliest recollections of listening to sports on the radio involved Duquesne basketball. Joe Tucker called the games in the late '40s and early '50s when I started following Duquesne basketball. I marveled at the way Joe could describe the action so that I could visualize what was happening on the court.

One of the things Joe did was to give footage on shots. It was Ricketts with a ten-foot hook, or Green, a 15-foot jumper.

After graduating from Duquesne in 1958 I was fortunate enough to land a job as the morning man at WDAD in Indiana, Pa., and also was able to start doing play-by-play on what was then Indiana State Teachers College basketball. ISTC later became Indiana State College, and then IUP, Indiana University of Pennsylvania.

And the Big Indians as they were known back then had excellent basketball teams. They played in tiny Waller Gym, capacity 900. We broadcast from Women's Athletic Director Ruth Podbielski's office overlooking the floor from one end, and you had to lean out to be able to see the play underneath the basket closer to the office. Waller would be packed for every game. In fact, some people who couldn't find standing room where they could get a glimpse of the floor, forgot about getting a seat, and would make their way up the steps to our office perch and stand behind us and lean out. Many times during a time-out I would lean back and bump into fans who would smile and say, "Pardon me."

In my first year doing the games we had a thrilling finish with Indiana scoring a last-second basket to notch the victory. Naturally the crowd went wild and, not to be outdone, I went ballistic, thinking I had done a great job of describing the action and conveying the excitement of the moment.

The next morning as I was walking downtown in Indiana, Joe Kozusko, the owner of Jo-Kay's Restaurant, greeted me.

"Exciting game last night, huh Ray?" he smiled.

"Yea, sure was," I beamed.

"I was ready to go to bed," said Joe, "and was actually lying

down when I heard the end of the game. I jumped out of bed because you were so excited. I figured Indiana had won because of all the excitement, but I had to wait a while until you came down a little bit and recapped what happened."

JOE KOZUSKO

Here's Joe behind the counter at his popular Jokay's Restaurant in Indiana, PA, in the 50's. Joe was the one who called to my attention that while it's okay to get excited broadcasting a game, you still have to communicate to the listener what's happening. He did it kindly and I appreciated it.

My heart sank a little. "Do you think I got too excited?" I asked.

"Well," Joe began, trying to soften the blow, "perhaps you could tone it down a bit and remember it's important that the listener knows what's happening. Your enthusiasm is good but remember you're not a fan."

I think I thanked Joe for his critique.

Later I realized how right he was, but it took quite a while before I became more detached from doing the game. I would say it was 20 years before I became more comfortable with highly charged games. I still get quite enthusiastic but hopefully not at the expense of the listener wondering what happened.

Another listener I listen to is Tom Burgunder. Tom is a Duquesne graduate and lifelong fan. Tom is also blind. So he not only listens carefully to Duquesne road games but also the home games, which he regularly attends.

Of course we talk quite often about Duquesne basketball, and Tom isn't bashful about critiquing my play-by-play. One thing he taught me years ago concerns the situation when the Dukes, for example, make two substitutions and I say "Gaydon and Higgins come in for the Dukes for Hudson and McAllister." Tom told me that's good, but then you have to tell me which players are now on the floor for Duquesne. Tom says it's important for the listener to know the five players who are on the floor. And you know what, he's right.

But the listener I listen to most is myself.

I live 55 miles from the Palumbo Center, Duquesne's home court. And I tape every game on a cassette recorder for two reasons. You never know when something so dramatic happens that you'll want to use it as a replay; and, besides, I want to critique my work. And I am very critical.

For example, am I using one word too much?

Once, when driving home from a Duquesne game, I popped the cassette recording of the game I had just broadcast into the tape player. Thinking I had done a pretty good job of describing the action, I listened in amazement as I heard myself using the word "flip" numerous times.

It was "Pipkins flips the ball to Jones, who flips it to Scott." A few seconds later, there was the word "flip" again.

Until I actually heard the tape, I never would have imagined that I had used the word "flip" that many times. Not that there's anything wrong with using the word "flip" occasionally, but there are so many other choices, for example, "passes" or "gives" or simply "Pipkins to Jones."

I immediately determined that in the next game I would use the word "flip" sparingly, if at all.

I not only listen to my tapes after games to try to do a better job, but I'm always tuning in to other games to hear how other play-by-play announcers call games. And of course I'm critical but I also listen for things they do that sound good, and invariably I'll incorporate some of their lingo or description into my play-by-play.

I was once told that if you copy one thing someone does that's almost like stealing, but if you take many things from others, that's research. Obviously I've been doing research for a long time, and it all goes back to when I listened to Joe Tucker giving footage on shots.

18

GULF WAR GAME

Tom Burgunder called me in the morning of Jan. 16th, 1991, to inform me, "You're not going to broadcast the Temple game tonight."

"What do you mean, Tom?" I asked.

"Well, you know what's going on over in the Gulf and KQV will definitely go with round-the-clock coverage if the Gulf War starts as early as this evening, which it looks like it will," Tom explained.

"I really hadn't thought about it, Tom, but don't worry, if we're not on the air, I'll come down and call the game for you," was my response.

TOM BURGUNDER
One of Duquesne's most ardent basketball fans. Being blind doesn't slow him down a bit. He bowls, rows, skis, and has run marathons, and is my number one listener who's not reluctant to point out my errors, always in a constructive manner.

Tom is a Duquesne graduate and an avid fan. Tom is also blind, but that doesn't slow him down a bit. He's a lawyer who has run a marathon, and he is also a cross-country skier.

And even though he could stay home and listen to the Duquesne games, Tom is a long-time season ticket holder because he enjoys the atmosphere of the games.

Shortly before airtime that night, we got the word from KQV that they were cancelling the broadcast of the game to give the war full-time coverage. Tom Burgunder was right. So I headed down to the stands and found a seat behind my friend Tom.

I did play-by-play for Tom, albeit in a more casual manner,

with more candid type observations and opinion on the goings-on. Tom would offer his comments and before long I realized that not only was Tom listening to my play-by-play but so were others within earshot. During one time-out a fan sitting in front of Tom turned and introduced himself, noting that he'd been away for 12 years, and was visiting from Los Angeles with his wife. He told me he used to listen to me all the time.

He continued, "And here I come back and you're right behind me. I'm really enjoying it."

The Dukes went on to win the game 60-59 in overtime, a big upset over a Temple team that was coached by the legendary John Chaney and featured future NBA player Mark Macon.

The next day I received a phone call from Brian O'Neill, a columnist for the *Pittsburgh Press*. He explained who he was, but that wasn't really necessary. I was quite familiar with his columns that were prominently featured four times weekly in the *Press* and were very popular.

Brian told me that a friend of his, Alex Melon, had called him to tell him about my personal play-by-play of the night before for Tom Burgunder. Alex was the public address announcer for the Duquesne games and someone I had gotten to know over the years.

Brian said he had already talked to Tom Burgunder about the column he was writing concerning the game and my play-by-play. I remember telling him that it wasn't any big deal, but he thought it would make a good column anyhow.

So we proceeded to talk about the personal broadcast and the next day when I got my copy of the *Press*, there was this full-blown article titled, "Dukes basketball announcer scores for a blind fan."

The article quoted both Tom and me with background information on both of us. Tom was quite complimentary of my play-by-play and noted the friendship that had developed between us over the years. The column even included the quote from the fan who was visiting from Los Angeles. Naturally I was pleased with the article.

But that wasn't the end of it. Carl Kologie, a Duquesne graduate whom I've known ever since our days together at Duquesne, just happened to be attending the Temple game. Carl also at the time was an Assistant Editor at the *Indiana Gazette*, the local Indiana newspaper, and in his story the next day, titled "Where were you when the shooting started?" included a couple of paragraphs about my personal play-by-play.

Then, Bill Hastings, who writes a popular weekly column in the *Indiana Gazette*, titled, "Inside Indiana," also mentioned the broadcast.

The following week the Dukes were on the road in Washington, D.C., to meet George Washington. On the morning of the game when I came down to breakfast, Head Coach John Carroll greeted me with, "Hey, Ray, you're famous. You made the *USA Today*."

I had no idea what he was talking about until he handed me the sports page which also had a clip about the broadcast. It was titled, "The Show Goes On," and mentioned of course the personal broadcast and quoted Burgunder with saying, "He (Ray) did the play-by-play. I supplied the reaction." Talk about getting maximum exposure over something I really felt was nothing out of the ordinary.

The best line about the experience came from Brian O'Neill, who wrote the original article that triggered the follow-ups. He used a quote I had given him to end his story when I told him that, "People were saying it was the best game I never broadcast."

19

THE PIRANHAS

In 1994 Pittsburgh was awarded a franchise in the Continental Basketball Association, the CBA, and that team became the Pittsburgh Piranhas.

When I read the announcement that there was going to be a pro basketball team in Pittsburgh, I immediately realized that someone would be broadcasting the team's games on the radio. *Why couldn't that someone be me?* I mused.

So I found out where to send my tape and resume and, lo and behold, I received a phone call from a man who identified himself as Tony Girdano, the Sports Director for WYJZ, the Pittsburgh radio station that would be airing the games. I remember the first thing Tony said to me, "Are you seriously interested in doing the Piranhas' games?"

"Of course," I replied, "that's why I sent in a tape and resume."

Tony went on, "But you've done the Duquesne games for years. Would you give them up?"

"Well," I allowed, "I was hoping that I could do both the Dukes and the Piranhas. I figured since the Piranhas will be playing at Palumbo (the home court of the Dukes) they obviously both can't be playing home games at the same time, so I thought there might not be too many conflicts."

Tony explained that he had been put in charge of finding the play-by-play person for the games and that, as he had attended Duquesne in the '70s, he was quite familiar with my play-by-play work.

Wow, for once I caught a break, I thought.

Then he continued. "The only problem is that they want someone to do all their games and there will obviously be some conflicts when the Piranhas are on the road and the Dukes are playing at the same time."

Long story short. Tony faxed me a Piranhas' schedule and I put it together with the Duquesne schedule and figured I could do 40 plus games of the Piranhas' 56-game schedule plus of course all of the Dukes' games.

Tony was able to sell the Piranhas on the arrangement, by volunteering himself to do the few games I could not make.

Thus began a season of virtually non-stop basketball, something I thoroughly enjoyed and look back on even now with fond memories.

The first game of the season pitted the Piranhas against Hartford in Connecticut on November 19, 1994, and the season ended 81 games later when the Piranhas played and lost the sixth game of the CBA Championship in Yakima, Washington on May 1, 1995.

Because I was constantly going from Piranhas' games to Duquesne games and back to the Piranhas, etc., the travel at times became rather hectic.

To give you an idea, here's how the season started.

On November 18th we flew to Hartford where the Piranhas played the Hellcats on the afternoon of the 19th followed by a flight back to Pittsburgh. The 20th was a day off. On the 21st the Piranhas hosted Quad City, and the 22nd found us flying to Fort Wayne for a game against the Fury on the 23rd. On the 24th it was a flight to Harrisburg for a game against the Hammerheads on the 25th. An early flight on the 26th took us from Harrisburg to Chicago to meet the Rockers that night. The 27th we flew back to Pittsburgh, and, amazingly there was no game that day. On the 28th Duquesne hosted Richmond; on the 29th Rockford visited the Piranhas, and Penn State was at Duquesne on the 30th. Then, thankfully, there were two days without a game.

So the season opened with this scorecard: in 13 days there were eight games in five different cities; four days were spent traveling, with one day off.

But I loved it. However, in January the breakneck schedule caught up with me in an unexpected manner.

I awoke shortly after midnight to the shock that my heartbeat was racing. When I took my pulse, I discovered that my heart was beating 120 times per minute. But that wasn't all. There seemed to occur a skip after every two rapid beats.

Naturally I was frightened. I had never experienced anything like this before. At first I thought it was only temporary and hoped that in a few minutes my heartbeat would return to normal. But that was not the case.

After about a half-hour I left the bedroom and lay down on the couch in the living room. As the racing and skipping heartbeats continued, my anxiety mounted. After another hour or so Dee realized I was no longer in bed and came down to check on me. When I told her what was happening she wanted me to get to the emergency room. There's no doubt that I should have done just that, but, you see, I had a Piranhas game in Pittsburgh that night, and I felt certain that if I showed up at "Emergency," I would be admitted to the hospital and submitted to a battery of tests. I could only imagine now many days that would take.

I tried to fall asleep; but the racing heartbeat continued until sunup. When I got up from the couch, I was dead tired, but, even though the missing beats persisted, my heartbeat had returned to near normal.

I did manage to see my chiropractor, Dr. David Grossi, whom I knew to be very knowledgeable in matters that extended beyond regular chiropractic care, and who was someone whose opinion I could trust. He checked me out and recommended some additional magnesium for my heart but also said I should be examined by a cardiologist. I thanked him and knew I would eventually follow his advice.

I tried to rest as much as I could during the day before driving to Pittsburgh around four p. m. for the game that night. I remember carrying my radio equipment from the Palumbo Center parking lot to the arena, and I remember that it had never felt so heavy. I was huffing and puffing as I made my way inside the arena, and I knew my heart was racing once again. On top of that, I literally felt as if I were floating, that is my feet were not touching the ground. I know that's impossible but that's what the erratic heartbeat caused me to feel.

Once the game started I guess the adrenaline kicked in, for I was able to get through the game. But when it was over I realized how tired

I felt. I wondered whether I would be able to get back to the parking lot and drive all the way home to Indiana.

The next few days my problem wasn't so much the rapid heartbeats but what I called the pauses between beats which would occur after every two, then three, then five, then two beats. When I rested, the pauses weren't as frequent; so I tried to rest as much as possible before either driving or flying to games. But I felt very fatigued nearly all of the time, something that I had never experienced before.

I recall one Duquesne trip to Philadelphia when we left Pittsburgh on January 27, 1995, for two games. We stopped en route in Carlisle for lunch and as I walked across the highway to a restaurant I was so weary I wondered whether I could even make it there. When I got inside I thought I probably just needed something to eat, but I had to force myself to eat, and, if anything, food only increased my skipping heartbeat. Naturally I became even more anxious.

At this point you have to be wondering, *What is it with this guy? Is he crazy? He could drop dead any minute.*

All I can say in hindsight is I'd never do it again. I wouldn't wait as I did until after the season was over to get checked out. I guess it comes under the heading that I referred to previously, "You don't have to be crazy to be in radio, but it helps."

Nellie King, my broadcast partner on the Duquesne games, who himself had undergone heart surgery that included five bypasses, was so concerned about my condition that he began carrying my broadcast equipment to the games.

Once the Duquesne season was over (in early March) the schedule lightened up because all I had to do were the Piranhas' games, which meant I traveled with them and there were more days off. When I was doing both Duquesne and Piranhas' games, I would have to arrange my own schedule much of the time. For example, I was in Shreveport, Louisiana for a Piranhas' game one night and then in Piscataway, New Jersey, the next day for a Duquesne game that night. The travel was hectic, to say the least, and that was a major cause of my problem, as I found out later when the season was over and I finally went to a cardiologist. In a word, my problem was caused by stress.

Not that the problem completely went away. After much testing it was determined that I had a condition called premature ventricular contractions, or PVC's. Nearly everyone, I was told, has PVC's from time to time, and, generally speaking, they're nothing to be concerned about. However, when they occur with the frequency I was experiencing and continue for lengthy periods, they just really sap your energy. I can certainly attest to that.

Over the past thirteen years since that original experience I've had some other incidents, not nearly as bad, and I've learned to live with the condition and keep it pretty much under control by taking a calcium channel blocker. I do not like to take any kind of medication, but in this case I'm only too happy to swallow the pills, thankful that they're doing the job.

And, hopefully, I've learned my lesson. Even now if I jam too much activity into three or four days in a row, the PVC's will increase and I know I've got to slow down. It helps greatly that I'm basically retired and during basketball season doing only 35 to 40 games instead of the 81 I did in the 94–95 season.

Since being diagnosed with PVC some thirteen years ago, I have also developed another irregular heartbeat called atrial fibrillation, and have had a pacemaker implanted to help normalize my heartbeat. So far, so good.

The Piranhas, by the way, even though they played for the CBA Championship in their first year of existence, folded after only one year. That meant of course that I didn't have to make a decision on what to do the next basketball season.

As I look back on this experience now, who knows, the death of the Piranhas may have saved my life.

20

THREE GAMES IN 24 HOURS

The 81 basketball games I broadcast during the 1994–95 season produced some hectic times on the road. Getting from one site to another often turned out to be quite a hassle.

One trip had me driving from Indiana, Pa., to South Bend, Indiana, for a Duquesne-Notre Dame game. The next morning I drove from South Bend to Fort Wayne, Indiana, for a Piranhas–Ft. Wayne contest. The next morning it was a long trek from Ft. Wayne to Olean, New York, for the Dukes' next game, which was against St. Bonaventure. Fortunately that game wasn't until the following day. So it was three games in four days, with 1100 plus miles of driving. I chose to drive rather than fly because logistically it made more sense and the roads were not expected to be snow-covered that February.

But by far the most challenging scenario occurred when I did three games in 24 hours in two different cities.

The Piranhas played the Rockers in Chicago on a Friday night. That was no problem. But Duquesne had a home game at the Palumbo Center in Pittsburgh the next day at noon while the Piranhas would play the same Chicago Rockers at Palumbo on Saturday night.

Both teams would be leaving Chicago in mid-morning, but I had to get an earlier flight, at six a. m. from Midway Airport in Chicago instead of O'Hare.

On Friday I checked with the concierge about getting an early morning cab around 4:30. "No problem at that time, "he said.

Early Saturday morning after no more than three hours' sleep I went down to the lobby and of course there was no concierge on duty that early. So I went outside to look for a cab. You could have shot a cannon down Michigan Avenue at that hour and not hit anything. I waited five minutes or so and nary a car, let alone a cab, passed by. Back into the hotel I went. I asked the clerk behind the desk whether he could call me a cab.

"No problem," he said. "Go out front and one should be there in five or ten minutes." It was now about 4:45 a. m. as I began my wait. Five minutes went by, then ten, then 15 and I was starting to panic. At 5:05 a cab came down Michigan Avenue and I frantically waved it to stop. The driver pulled over and I told him I had to be at Midway as soon as possible. He loaded my luggage and broadcast equipment into the trunk as I jumped into the back seat.

Before the driver could get into the front seat, someone knocked on my window. It was the clerk from the hotel.

I rolled down my window to hear him say, "This isn't the cab company I called." Without hesitation I said, "I'm sorry. This is the first cab that came. Yours isn't here yet and I have a flight to catch."

The driver took off and fortunately there was no traffic at all on an early Saturday morning as he raced to Midway. We got there at 5:40 a.m.

Since this was long before 9–11, it took just a few minutes to get to my gate and I boarded the plane with ten minutes to spare. I had arranged with my wife Dee to pick me up at the Pittsburgh Airport because I still didn't have a lot of time to spare, and six a. m. Chicago time is seven a. m. in Pittsburgh. So when we landed it was already 8:20, and by the time I got my luggage and radio equipment it was pushing nine a. m.

Because it's only a 30-minute drive from the airport to Pittsburgh, I told Dee, "I think we have time for breakfast."

We stopped at an Eat n-Park and we parked in the back of the lot so that I could change into the clothes that Dee had brought me for the Duquesne game. I did this in the front seat of the car, constantly looking out the window in my ridiculous modesty to see whether anyone was nearby.

After breakfast we set out for Palumbo, arriving at 11 a. m. I hooked up the broadcast equipment and proceeded to call the game. When it was over we headed to a nearby hotel at which we had a reservation. After taking the shower that I really needed and a brief rest, we had a quick dinner and it was back to Palumbo for the

Piranhas–Rockers game at seven p. m.

At around 11 p. m. when my head hit the pillow at the hotel, my mind was still buzzing with names, numbers, and basketball from the three games I had just broadcast in two different cities in 24 hours.

As noted before, it has been said that you don't have to be crazy to be in radio, but it helps. Obviously sanity isn't one of my strong suits.

21

THE BUS TO ROCKFORD

One of the more unusual experiences I had during the 1994-95 basketball season occurred when I had to fly from Pittsburgh to Rockford, Illinois, for a Piranhas' game. Ordinarily I tried to go with the Piranhas because that made it a lot easier but when Duquesne games happened in between, which was more than half the time, I had to make my own arrangements.

I glanced at my tickets as I was leaving Pittsburgh and couldn't quite make sense of the timing. It appeared that the flight from Chicago to Rockford was going to take an hour and 25 minutes, and instead of questioning further, I assumed that since there was an hour difference between Pittsburgh and Chicago, that perhaps the ticket reflected the hour difference in the flight from Chicago to Rockford. I should have realized that instead of adding an hour to my flight an hour should be subtracted going from the east to the midwest.

After landing at O'Hare in Chicago I started the trek to my next gate thinking I had over an hour before my flight. As I casually approached my gate figuring I had at least 45 minutes to read the current *Sports Illustrated*, the ticket agent said, "Are you Mr. Goss?"

Now that caught me completely by surprise. How would the ticket agent have any idea who I was. "Well, yes I am," I replied curiously. "How do you know who I am?"

"Well, you're the last person unaccounted for, and if you're ready to go so are we," the pleasant ticket agent smiled.

I just couldn't imagine a plane taking off nearly an hour ahead of time. "You mean, the plane is ready to go as soon as I board?" I responded.

"Plane, what do you mean, plane? You're taking the bus to Rockford," the agent stated. "Did you think you were flying?"

"Well, this is an airport, isn't it? What do you mean bus?" I responded incredulously.

"Oh you didn't know. They recently grounded all the smaller Midwest planes that normally go from places like Chicago to Rockford because one of the planes had a problem, and until they get the green light from the FAA, we're substituting buses for these short flights."

I couldn't help laughing. That explained why it was going to take an hour and 25 minutes to navigate the 70 miles to Rockford. And the bus would take the passengers to the Rockford airport, just as an airplane would.

I walked down the steps at O'Hare and out the door and there was the bus, parked not 50 yards away. I was still smiling as I boarded and discovered I was the third and final passenger on the trip.

It was the only time I ever went to the airport to catch a bus, but hey, it got me to the game on time, and that's the only thing that really mattered.

22

BEST REF I EVER SAW

RED MIHALIK
He was born to be a basketball referee, and virtually everyone who saw him call a game agreed that he was the best. I was privileged to see him officiate many games and to get to know him personally, which I count among my biggest thrills to this day.

Zigmund "Red" Mihalik was the best basketball referee I ever saw.

And I'm not alone in my opinion. *Dell Publications* in 1951 named him the best referee in the United States. They described him as "having a fetish for fairness, without being whistle happy, being mentally alert, in good physical condition, and in good officiating position 99% of the time."

Red officiated six NCAA Championship Finals, three NAIA and three NIT Finals, and the Tokyo and Mexico City Olympics in 1964 and '68.

Red did games at every level and was not above doing junior high games even when he had hit the so-called "big time," that being major college basketball conferences like the ACC and Big Ten.

He loved the game of basketball and the young men and women who played it. Even though there was never any doubt about who was in charge when he called a game, Red treated the players with respect and would talk to them privately during the game, basically teaching them what they were allowed or not permitted to do on the court so he wouldn't have to blow his whistle.

And he was always cordial and friendly to me. I would see Red after games or on flights as we headed to various games and, naturally, we would talk basketball.

Red had a passion for the game. He was always watching games when he wasn't officiating, which wasn't often, since he was in such high demand.

That doesn't mean everyone liked Red or agreed with how he called a specific game. There were coaches who didn't want him on their home games, because Red was definitely not a "homer."

These same coaches didn't mind having Red on the road because he would "call them as he saw them."

After a game at old Waller Gym on the Indiana State College campus in the early '60s, Peck McKnight, the coach at Indiana, paid a visit to the officials' dressing room after his team had lost a close game that Red officiated. Peck was still noticeably upset over his team's loss and proceeded to berate Red and went into great detail on how Red supposedly missed a couple of calls that cost his team the game. After pontificating for several minutes, Peck stopped to catch his breath, and Red said, "Are you finished, Peck?"

Wearily, Peck replied, "Yeh, I guess so."

And Red responded, "Good, because I have Duke and North Carolina tomorrow night and I have an early flight so I have to get going."

I can recall broadcasting many games that Red officiated and thinking afterwards *I don't think there was one call that Red made that I disagreed with.* And how many times can anyone make that statement?

Of course, once in a while, Red like anyone in any walk of life would make a bad call, or at least make a call that seemed bad.

I remember a game between IUP and California State College in California, Pa. Jack Benedict and I were calling the game on WDAD, from a position above the court, a spot I preferred because you get a good overall view of the floor without being screened out from time to time.

Red made a call in the game that I consider to be the best I've ever seen.

It occurred in the second half when the ball was deflected out of bounds right in front of the Indiana bench. Red happened to be positioned there and as the ball zipped past him, he turned to retrieve it. A player on the Indiana bench tossed him the ball and Red authoritatively (he was always authoritative on his calls) pointed to the left and started to hand the ball to an Indiana player, who seemed to hesitate as he stepped out of bounds to accept the ball. The California players also hesitated, before slowly retreating to go on defense.

I remember thinking, *Oh, oh, Red missed that one.* I definitely felt an Indiana player had touched the ball last before it went out of bounds.

And even though it appeared to be a blatant error, no one challenged it, certainly not the Indiana coaches or players who would benefit from the miscue, but neither did the California players or coaches, an obvious testimony to the high regard both teams and coaches had for Red.

Then just as he was preparing to hand the ball to the Indiana player to inbound it, Red pulled it away and tooted his whistle not once, not twice, but three times, the shrill, piercing tone echoing throughout the gym and bringing the overflow crowd to silence.

Red then bellowed for everyone to hear, including Jack and me, even though we had headsets on which normally block out the crowd. "Hold it, hold it," Red began, "my fault, it's this way," as he pointed dramatically to his right, indicating California ball.

I remember smiling to myself and thinking, "*Well, Red almost blew one.*" Indiana dutifully retreated on defense, and California took the ball inbounds with nary a peep coming from the Indiana coaches on the reversal of the call.

About two weeks later I ran into Red at the airport. After exchanging pleasantries, I just had to ask him about his call reversal in the IUP–California game.

Red was not only dramatic on the court with his calls, but could also be in person when discussing something important. "Ray," he began, "I had to change that call. You see when the ball went out of bounds I turned around to retrieve it and lost my sense of direction. I knew it was California's ball, but I pointed the wrong way. As I was about to hand the ball to the Indiana player, I realized I had pointed the wrong way, so I just changed the call."

I smiled broadly at Red's explanation. Knowing him, had he not changed the call and realized later that he had made a mistake, he would probably lie awake all night agonizing over his error. He was that scrupulously honest.

It wasn't a controversial call in an important high profile game that determined the outcome, but in my estimation, it was the best call I've ever seen an official make.

Late in life Red was honored by his hometown of Ford City, Pa., when the high school gym was named after him.

And Red was elected to the National Basketball Hall of Fame in 1986, an honor he reluctantly accepted, because he was such a humble person.

IUP Athletic Director Herm Sledzik approached Red about the Hall of Fame, asking him to fill out the necessary papers for possible nomination. When Red refused, not surprisingly, Herm filled them out for him, and one of the accompanying letters supporting his nomination came from none other than North Carolina Coach Dean Smith.

I recall congratulating him at an IUP game he was attending shortly after he received the honor. He squirmed and told me how uncomfortable he felt about the induction. I asked him to join me at halftime for an interview and he politely declined, saying, "Ray, don't take this personally, but I just don't feel comfortable talking about myself." I didn't push him. I smiled and accepted his decision.

It was several years later when Red was winding down his long, illustrious career that I talked to him again at an IUP game he was attending. Red's back was really hurting. He had injured it originally when he was officiating a game and while making a call, stepped awkwardly off the edge of a raised court and felt something "go" in his back. Even though he was in great pain, he finished the game. And he continued to do games that season even though his back was "killing" him. Reluctantly he finally received treatment, but his back was never again the same, and Red started cutting back on his schedule, even though he was still in demand.

It came to the point when Red felt he just wasn't at his best, that he couldn't move quickly enough to get into position to make calls, and he would agonize afterwards if he felt his lack of mobility caused him perhaps to miss a call or to make the wrong call.

Eventually he quit officiating but would still volunteer to work some junior high games so that he could teach the youngsters about his life's passion, the game of basketball.

Red still liked to attend as many games as he could, and when I saw him at another IUP game, I tried one more time to get an interview with him, this time simply saying, "Red, would you consider taping a short interview with me for use at halftime?"

He paused for a moment, then said, "Ray, you know how I don't like to do interviews, but because it's you, I'll do it."

He made me feel like a million bucks, and the interview was terrific. Once you got Red telling stories, they turned out to be just as good as his officiating, in other words, simply great.

When Red died on September 25, 1996, basketball lost one of its most energetic and colorful personalities, and perhaps the greatest basketball official ever; and everybody who knew Red personally lost a dear friend.

23

"NO BASKET"

Over the past 50 years I've broadcast at least 2,000 basketball games. Yet I can count on one hand the number of times an official's call at the very end of the game absolutely decided the outcome.

I'm thinking particularly of a ruling that either allows or disallows a field goal as the buzzer is sounding.

A ruling one way and Team A wins; the opposite ruling and it's Team B that is victorious. No call elicits more controversy than the "good" or "no good" call when an official has to decide in a split second whether the ball left the shooter's hand before the buzzer sounded and the clock showed three zeroes.

Today that call is reviewable in the NBA and in many major college basketball conferences where officials have access to instant replay.

In 1977 in a game between IUP and California State College, the ruling official didn't have the luxury of instant replay on a last-second shot.

The official was Eddie Plank, a veteran whistle tooter, who is not only one of the nicest guys you'd ever meet, but an excellent, well respected basketball referee.

Many officials have outgoing personalities, which isn't surprising given the nature of their demanding and high-profile profession. Eddie wasn't like that. He was quiet and unassuming, but very likeable and always pleasant to me when we'd chat before or after a game he was working.

EDDIE PLANK
A tremendous basketball official and nice guy to boot. Maybe he missed a call, but hey, that's what got him in this book. Thanks, Eddie.

On this particular occasion at a packed IUP gym for the Indians' home conference opener against rival California, the game came down to the wire. With 21 seconds to go, Gerry Rectenwald, IUP's point guard, drove the lane and sank a four-footer to give IUP a 74-73 lead.

Cal, without a timeout remaining, pushed the ball up the floor and got the ball to Delmore Beshore, a prolific scorer and Cal's top offensive threat. But Beshore missed a baseline jumper. The ball found its way into Cal's hands for one more chance. With three seconds to go, Cal's Dick Hartung wound up with the ball 25 feet from the basket right in front of the Cal bench. He knew he had to let if fly to beat the clock and a second later his 25-foot jumper was in the air.

I remember vividly my call (and since I also have it on tape I've been able to review it many times), particularly the part when the ball was midway in flight. I had time to take a quick glance at the game clock above the IUP basket. It showed one second, meaning "good if it goes."

A split second later and the ball swished cleanly through the net. The buzzer must have sounded simultaneously but no one could hear it because the gym had been and continued to be sheer bedlam from the time of Rectenwald's go-ahead basket.

As soon as the ball went through the net though, the crowd's enthusiasm was snuffed out immediately and silence consumed the packed field house. At least 98% of the crowd were IUP fans, and they instantly realized that IUP had lost a heartbreaker on a buzzer-beater by Cal.

But wait, Eddie Plank, the trailing official near mid-court, had yet to make the call to signal officially that the basket was indeed "good."

And, incredibly, after just a moment's hesitation, Eddie was waving his hands from side to side, ruling, "no basket!"

On seeing Eddie's ruling, I shifted gears. "Eddie Plank ruled no basket, he ruled no basket, etc., etc."

The fans were stunned. They went from elation when Rectenwald's basket apparently gave IUP the win, to dejection when Hartung's basket apparently gave California the victory, to utter disbelief at Eddie Plank's call that restored the win for IUP.

More than a few fans seated in front of our broadcast position high above the floor at mid-court turned to Jack and me to get our reaction and when we both indicated by the up and down movements of our heads accompanied by the "basket was good" signal, they also nodded their heads confirming our reaction.

It seemed that virtually everyone in IUP's gym knew the basket was good, except one person; but that one person, Eddie Plank, was the only one who counted.

IUP had won 74-73 on Eddie Plank's decisive call.

As soon as California realized victory had been snatched from them, Beshore went ballistic and raced after Eddie Plank, either to protest the call or to do who knows what? I'm not sure which because Cal's Coach Myles Witchey was also headed in Plank's direction, and, fortunately, Witchey was able to intercept Beshore with a bear hug before Delmore could reach Eddie.

Over the years I've wondered about that call. Anyone can miss a call. *Perhaps*, I thought, *Eddie Plank didn't hear the buzzer*, which was understandable, given the noise in the gym. But if that were the case, Eddie could have checked with the timer before making his ruling. Of course the timer was IUP's Ed Receski and he would have to make the critical ruling.

Or perhaps Eddie just lost track of the time on the clock and simply with a 50-50 choice facing him, made the wrong one.

When I picture in my mind's eye the scene on the floor as Eddie Plank made his call, I can still see someone else in the picture. It's Carl Davis, the IUP coach.

Carl, like many coaches, was generally animated on the bench. To say he was "into the game" would be an understatement. And in this case with the game on the line, Carl was fully at mid-court, waving his arms from side to side, indicating that in his mind the basket was "no good."

Eddie Plank was no more than eight to ten feet from Davis and after that moment's hesitation perhaps he heard Carl trying to help him make the call.

Thirty years after the fact, Carl Davis recalled the game and particularly those last few frantic seconds as if it had all happened yesterday.

He confirmed the fact that he was "waving intensely" while yelling "no good, no good." Did that possibly influence Eddie Plank's call? After all, the two knew each other well. Carl said, "I can't say."

And what is Eddie Plank's recollection of the call?

Eddie's first comment, when I asked him whether he remembered the game and the call, was, "I sure do."

He went on to say "I don't know what happened to me. I was astonished when it went in. It was so darn close. I think about that so many times."

He allowed that he was good friends with both Carl Davis, the IUP coach, and Myles Witchey, the Cal coach. And he said, "Myles came into the dressing room after the game. He was really upset with me."

When I told Eddie that my recollection of the call included the fact that Carl Davis was quite close to Eddie when he made the call and Carl told me he was waving intensely that it wasn't a good basket and simultaneously shouting "no basket, no basket," Eddie responded by saying he wasn't aware that Carl was that close.

He did say that when he went to the scorer's table right after the game, Ed Receski, the official timer, told him "you were right" meaning he made the correct call. Of course I must point out that Receski was an IUP employee and very loyal to the school.

Eddie Plank not only officiated basketball games at the Division II level of the NCAA but worked for the then ECAC and did many Division 1 games, including contests that involved ACC teams. In other words, Eddie was extremely well thought of and respected in college basketball officiating circles, and if he did miss that one call, well it certainly does nothing to diminish his outstanding career as a basketball official.

24

WHEN YOU GOTTA GO

Who hasn't faced this dilemma? You passed the last rest stop on the highway, it's at least a half-hour before the next one and even though five minutes ago you were okay, now all of a sudden, you "gotta go."

Now just imagine what a broadcaster goes through when he's announcing a game, and he's on the air continuously for anywhere from two and a half to three hours and you begin to get an idea of what he experiences.

I learned a long time ago to be very careful how much water I consume during the course of a game. But when you're uttering thousands of words broadcasting a game, you just have "to wet your whistle" from time to time.

The key is to sip a bit of water when needed. But that doesn't always work. You just never know when nature might call and when she does, especially in the middle of a game, well, the end of the game can never come too soon.

I remember an IUP game at Miller Stadium in Indiana. Jack Benedict and I were broadcasting the game and Doug Steve was doing the sideline reports. I wasn't too much concerned about how much water I consumed because Jack always handled the halftime interview, which allowed me to take a mid-game break.

But the second half of this particular game required a lot more time than usual and as the end of the contest slowly approached I found myself squirming more and more and urging "whatever gods there be" to hasten the ending.

Once the game finally ended, I still had to endure the post-game show, which included on-the-field interviews with IUP Coach Frank Cignetti and the players of the game. While Jack Benedict was making his way down to the field to join Doug Steve for the post-game, I recapped the game, knowing I would have a six-or seven-minute break once the interviews began.

No problem, I thought. That gives me plenty of time to dash down the steps and make it to the men's room and get back in time to close out the broadcast.

Of course fans were still leaving the stands after the game; so it took two or three precious minutes to reach ground level. By the time I had completed my visit to the men's room, another couple of minutes had elapsed. Meanwhile I was listening to the interviews on the radio and felt I still had plenty of time to get back to the booth.

But by the time I was hustling back up the stadium steps I heard Jack complete his interview with "and now let's go back to Ray Goss in the booth."

Well not yet I thought as I was now bounding up the steps two at a time. Maybe as many as fifteen seconds of dead air occurred before I breathlessly intoned, "Thanks Jack, and we'll be back to wrap things up right after this break on 1160 WCCS."

As the commercial aired, I just leaned back and thought, *well at least I feel a lot better.*

Several years ago, I broadcast the WPIAL Class A Championship football game on WTYM, Kittanning. The game was played at Three Rivers Stadium in Pittsburgh and the hospitality was first class.

The game began at noon and the stadium folk had prepared a full-course breakfast buffet for the media. I had a private booth and even though I was doing the game by myself I had already scoped out the location of the men's room, which was just steps away from my booth.

I also knew I would have a five or six-minute break at halftime when WTYM would do a news update from the station.

Everything was fine until midway through the fourth quarter when the "urge to go" began and then intensified more quickly than usual.

The game was close and I knew there would be several time-outs before the game ended. I didn't have to do a long post-game show, just a quick wrap-up, but I was squirming more than ever, wondering if I would ever make it to the end of the game.

That's when I made a quick decision. During a time-out with two and a half minutes to go, I called for a 60-second break and bolted for the rest room.

I had the presence of mind to start my stopwatch as I headed out of the booth. While in the men's room I kept a wary eye on my watch as the seconds ticked by: 25, 30, 35, 40, and I wasn't quite ready to return to the booth. At 52 seconds I zoomed out of the rest room and into the booth in a flash, slipping on my headset mike just as the commercial ended.

I hadn't missed a beat, and I couldn't help smiling as I enjoyed the great wave or relief I was experiencing.

Later as I drove from Three Rivers Stadium on my way to Brockway, Pa. for yet another football play-off game I was slated to broadcast that evening, I couldn't help thinking, *when you gotta go, you gotta go.*

25

AMTRAK TO PHILLY

NELLIE KING

I admired him from the stands when he pitched for the Pittsburgh Pirates and then was fortunate enough to work with him for 26 years when he did the color commentary on the Duquesne broadcasts.

Nellie King called me at 10:30 Friday morning, February 12th, 1983.

Nellie was the Sports Information Director at Duquesne and my partner on the Duquesne basketball broadcasts. Nellie also formerly pitched for nine years in the majors with the Pittsburgh Pirates, and broadcast Pirate baseball games with Bob Prince for nine years.

"The reason I'm calling," Nellie began, "is there's a snowstorm in the East that's blanketing Philadelphia and our flight has been cancelled. We're going to take the Amtrak train that leaves at noon from Pittsburgh."

"Well, I'd better hurry if I'm going to make it, Nellie," I told him.

A few minutes later I was on my way to Pittsburgh and fortunately was able to make the train with 20 minutes to spare.

The first part of the trip to Philly was uneventful, but as we approached Harrisburg the snow began to accumulate dramatically. Then it happened. Instead of pulling out of the Harrisburg station after a scheduled stop we were told there would be a delay because of the heavy snow accumulation just ahead.

For over an hour we did not budge one inch; and once we started again it wasn't long before we came to another unscheduled stop. This time we were delayed for nearly three hours.

Later I found out that word of our delay had reached the Pittsburgh media and that on the evening television news a report had aired about our train being stuck between Harrisburg and Philadelphia. My wife, Dee, told me that our eight-year-old son Jason was watching TV with her when he heard the news and that he began crying because he was concerned for his Dad's safety. Dee had had to assure him that I would be okay.

Meanwhile, after the train got rolling again it wasn't speeding along but creeping to our eventual destination. We finally reached the 30th Street Station in Philly at 12:30 a.m., more than 12 hours after leaving Pittsburgh. Because the game wasn't to be played until two o'clock Saturday afternoon, we were sure that we had plenty of time.

But when we recovered our luggage and found out that Philadelphia already had 20 inches of snow and that it was still snowing, we also discovered that there was no ground transportation whatsoever. So we began walking from the train station to our hotel, more than a mile away.

The snow was mid-thigh in many places, but we were able to find a path through the drifts most of the way, and because there were no cars at all on the road, we trudged along right in the middle of the street.

Of course many of us weren't properly dressed to wade through the snow. For example, Joey Myers, Duquesne's high-scoring senior forward, was wearing loafers and no socks.

As we walked along in single file, I had my luggage in one hand and my radio equipment in the other. Each of these items had to weigh 25 to 30 pounds. After a bit, Coach Jim Satalin said to me, "Ray, let me have that equipment for a while." Most grateful, I handed it right over.

By the time we got into the hotel and checked in it was nearly two a.m. Breakfast Saturday morning was at ten a.m. and that's when we found out that the buses were still not running. This meant we had to take the subway to Temple.

We checked out of the hotel, grabbed our luggage and headed to the subway station. We arrived at the Temple gym on Broad Street in plenty of time for the two o'clock tip-off.

Because of the snow the crowd was sparse, a condition which

would work in Duquesne's favor. The game went into overtime and the Dukes came up big in the extra five minutes to pull off an astonishing 73–70 upset win. The Red-and-Blue were led by unheralded Derrick Eaglin's career-high 21 points. Joey Myers, sick as a dog after the trek through the snow in loafers and no socks, gutted it out and contributed to the win.

Following the game we were told that as the airport was still closed, and it was back on the subway. We checked into another hotel in downtown Philly, hoping to catch an early morning flight to Pittsburgh.

At six in the morning we were wakened with some good news. We were able to rent three vans. Even though there was still plenty of snow in Philadelphia, the streets had improved some, and vehicles were able to move through the city.

We headed to the airport in our vans and after waiting more than two hours to get a flight, with no guarantee that we would even get a flight later in the day, a decision was made to go back to the city and take the train to Pittsburgh.

I was in the second van as we left the station. The roads were still icy when the van in front of ours spun around in an attempt to avoid an oncoming vehicle that was sliding towards it. I watched in amazement as the van did a complete 360, somehow avoiding the out-of-control vehicle in its path. Later, Nellie King, who was in that van, told me he told Duquesne's Andy Sisinni, who was seated next to him, "Andy, after that, nothing's going to happen to us now. We'll get back to Pittsburgh okay."

And we did, after another long train ride. At least we didn't get stalled en route. Just mention that trip to anyone from Duquesne who made it, and that person will immediately start recalling the incredible details, including the fact that after all was said and done, the Dukes had recorded a huge upset over the Temple Owls in overtime.

26

NEVER BEEN LATE

I've never been late or missed a game I was scheduled to broadcast. That's over 2,000, probably closer to 3,000 (knock on wood, since I'm still doing games).

There have been some close calls though.

One occurred when I was driving from my home in Indiana, Pa. to the Oakland section of Pittsburgh for the annual basketball battle between rivals Duquesne and Pitt on February 22, 1978.

It's only 55 miles and as usual I left early, just in case. Game time was 7:30 p. m. with air time 7:15.

At 5:25 I approached the Squirrel Hill Tunnels, only ten miles from Oakland. Suddenly the traffic slowed and quickly came to a complete stop. No problem. This has happened before and usually lasts only a few minutes.

This time 15 minutes elapsed and no one moved an inch. When people started getting out of their cars, I joined them to find out what was causing the delay. The word was that there was an accident in the tunnel and we'd have to wait until it was cleared.

"How long will that take?" I asked no one in particular.

"Who knows?" someone replied.

There was nothing to do but wait. Before long it was 6:30 and still no movement. I thought, *I would ordinarily be there by now, and I can just imagine what Mel Check, our engineer, and Nellie King, my broadcast partner, must be thinking.*

As I sat in my car nervously checking my watch, I figured *well this is it, the first game I'm either going to miss completely or at least be late for the tip-off.* And there was no way to let Nellie and Mel know about my predicament. This was long before cell phones.

Then at 6:40, without warning, the traffic started to move, slowly at first, then up to 15 and then 20 miles an hour. There was still time to make the tip-off and perhaps some of the pre-game show.

At seven p. m. I pulled into the media parking lot at the Pitt Field House. I rolled down my window and gave the attendant my name. "Sorry," he said. "There's no more room in the media lot."

"But isn't my name on the list?"

"Yes, but there's no more room. You'll have to park in the regular lot," he said, pointing right, up the hill.

I didn't argue. What good would it do. I backed out of the lot and headed up the hill. Naturally there was a line of cars ahead of me. By the time I parked and grabbed my bag, it was 7:10, five minutes until air time.

I ran down the hill heading for the "will call" window to get my media credentials. The gate was near the main entry to the Pitt Field House another couple hundred yards away. As I neared the student gate, I figured I'd try to get into the building there.

I said to the attendant, "I'm Ray Goss. I do the play-by-play for Duquesne and I'm running late. Can I get in here?"

The attendant looked at me, hesitated, then smiled and said, "I recognize your voice. Go ahead."

"Thanks," I said over my shoulder as I jogged to my courtside broadcast position, smiling to myself and musing, *sometimes it helps to be famous.*

Mel and Nellie greeted me simultaneously with "Where were you?"

"Accident in the Squirrel Hill Tunnels," I started to say when Mel interrupted me with "ten seconds to air."

Ten seconds later it was "This is Ray Goss along with Nellie King...." as if nothing out-of-the-ordinary had occurred.

_____

Then there was the game when I was so sick any sane person would have been in bed. I was slated to do the radio broadcast of the 1968 Dapper Dan Roundball Classic at the Civic Arena, an annual all-star matchup between the best high school seniors from Pennsylvania versus their counterparts from the rest of the United States.

Before the game I had talked to my Mom in Carnegie and accepted her invitation to dinner. I told her I'd have to eat early since I wanted to leave about five o'clock to get to the Arena.

"No problem," she said. "It will be good to see you. Get here early so we can visit."

"I'll be there by three, Mom."

On the drive down from Indiana, I felt as if I was "catching something." When I got out of the car in Carnegie and walked up the steps to my Mom's, I could tell I was weak, and not good at all. Of course my Mom could see right away I was ill.

"Lie down," she said. "You're not going anywhere tonight."

I didn't have the strength to argue with her, but deep down I knew that I had to go to the game. There was no substitute to call at this late hour.

I slept fitfully for the next hour or so and when I was able to make my way down to the kitchen, I told my Mom, "I'm going to take a shower and get ready for the game."

Of course she tried to talk me out of it, but I told her I was feeling somewhat better (not true).

"Then, after you shower, eat something," she said.

"Can't Mom, I don't have enough time," (also not true but I reasoned better to lie than try to argue with my Mother).

I drove to the Civic Arena, still feeling weak and nauseous. For this game, because I didn't have preferred parking, I had to park at the Chatham Center, down the hill from the Arena.

I took a deep breath as I started up the hill to the Arena. My breathing became more labored with each step and I had to stop several times, each time thinking, *this is crazy, I'm too sick and weak to even attempt this.*

But I persevered and as I entered the Arena I thought *I'm almost there.* I still had to climb the steps to my broadcast location. I remember saying to myself *if I can just make it up the steps to my spot, maybe I'll be okay.*

I finally plopped down in my seat and began wearily to prepare for the broadcast. I had made up my mind to just shove this illness aside until the game was over.

Somehow once we went on the air, I guess the adrenaline or whatever kicked in and I did the whole game without once thinking about how sick I was. I've always said that when I'm doing a game there really is no awareness of time. My concentration has to be focused entirely on the game moment by moment and I've rarely felt that a game took any time at all.

Anyhow, when the all-star game was over and we signed off I took a deep breath and thought, *now I can be sick*. But when I got up I realized I felt pretty good. In fact I was "okay," there was no weakness or feeling of nausea.

The old saying "mind over matter" had to be working for me that night.

I called my Mom to tell her I felt fine and that instead of staying in Carnegie with her that night I would be driving back home to Indiana. Naturally she objected. I fully expected that. After all she's a mother and that's what mothers do.

Then there was the game at Madison Square Garden on January 31, 1970, with the Dukes playing Long Island.

We arrived at MSG and had to take the elevator to the ninth level. Our broadcast position was in a gondola that hung from the roof of the Garden. The reason for the gondola for broadcasting we were told was that somehow the architects had failed to include broadcast positions in their plans. And, amazingly, I guess no one caught the omission because the Garden was built without them and the gondola was installed afterwards.

To get into the gondola, one had to climb a flight of steps that had to be operated electronically. Before the game they were positioned so the media could climb into the gondola. Once the game started the steps were raised so that they wouldn't obstruct the view of the spectators in that area.

When the first half of the Duquesne-LIU game was over and we went to commercial, John Cigna, my partner, who later would go on to be the popular morning man at KDKA Radio, asked me whether I was going to the press lounge.

"Yes," I said "I'm going to get a soda."

"Bring me back a Coke," John said, as he prepared to do his halftime interview.

JOHN CIGNA
One of my many "partners" on the Duquesne broadcasts. After working with me, the Brooklyn native chess player went on to become the very popular morning man at KDKA for may years, something for which I can take no credit whatsoever.

The steps from the gondola had been lowered for halftime and I made my way down and to the elevator. The press lounge was on the sixth level, about a quarter of the way around the building.

After talking to a couple of reporters from Pittsburgh who were covering the game, I grabbed a couple of Cokes and headed for the elevator. I knew I had six or seven minutes until the second half started, plenty of time.

I waited patiently for the elevator but it didn't come. I didn't even know where the steps were to get up the three flights to the gondola, but time was running short. Finally, after what seemed an eternity, but was probably only two or three minutes, the elevator doors opened. Then it seemed to take another minute or two for the elevator to get to the ninth level. I knew I'd be cutting it close, and I exited the elevator in a panic.

I looked to my left for the gondola. It wasn't there! How can that be? I went ballistic. Where had it gone? Then I looked to my right. Finally I spotted it, halfway around the Garden from where I was. I had gotten on the wrong elevator and was now at least 150 yards from the gondola. And to make matters worse, the second half was about to begin.

I took off running with a large cup of Coke in each hand splashing on me and the floor. About halfway to the gondola I took a look at the floor some 200 feet below, and indeed the second half was underway.

Now huffing and puffing I finally reached the base of the gondola, and yes, you guessed it, the steps had already been raised. There I was helplessly stranded in the stands with two Cokes dripping all over me.

The game was now into the second minute of the second half and there was John Cigna up there, having never done play-by-play in his life.

I started yelling to anyone up there in the gondola, although I couldn't see anyone because naturally they were watching the game. After a couple of "Hey, I'm supposed to be up there," someone spotted me and eventually someone else pushed a button and the gondola steps started to descend, slowly, very slowly. Thoughts of the old radio show "Inner Sanctum" crossed my mind as the steps creaked eerily downward.

Even before the steps were all the way down, I jumped on the first one. Cokes were cascading everywhere. I climbed as quickly as I could with the motorized steps still moving into their final position. Amazingly I didn't fall flat on my face. Of course the cups of Coke were now just half-filled.

I took my seat next to John who greeted me, right on the air, with "Ray, where were you?"

"Sorry, John," I said, "I took the wrong elevator."

The second half was nearly three minutes old when I resumed calling the play-by-play.

So there it is. I've never actually missed a game, despite some close calls. But I guess in the interest of accuracy, this chapter should be titled, "Never Been Late, Well, Almost Never."

27

CELL PHONE

How did we ever exist without cell phones?

I said the same thing when VCR's, microwaves, computers, fax machines, CD's, DVD's, etc., etc., became popular.

I've always been slow getting up to speed with anything that's new, anything that's supposed to make life easier. Cell phones were no exception. For many years I never felt I needed one. Then for Christmas several years ago our seven children bought my wife a cell phone and paid for the first year of service.

Dee hardly used it; so I started using it, and eventually it became mine. She used it on occasion and I've often asked her if she wanted me to get her her own, since really the one I was using was hers. She keeps saying she really has little use for one.

And the more I used the cell phone, the more uses I found for it.

When I broadcast the Duquesne basketball games, I use the cell phone as a means of communication in emergencies. Even though the equipment we use to broadcast the games is computerized and works beautifully nearly all the time, there are occasions when for reasons known only to the computer gods, the equipment fails. When that happens it means we go off the air, the worst possible thing that can happen to any broadcast.

In order to avoid or at least curtail these occasional mishaps, I began telling our operators at KQV to call me the moment we have on-air problems or actually go off the air. I told them the best and quickest way to get in touch with me is to call me on my cell phone, which I had clipped to my belt and which would vibrate when a call is coming in.

Even though you would think with the modern broadcasting equipment we have, we would know immediately if we were knocked off the air, that's not always the case. Even though there's a screen on the equipment which can tell us there's a problem, when you're focusing on broadcasting the game, your concentration is on the action and not on a screen on the equipment.

So whenever my cell phone vibrates the first thing I do is check the computer screen and if I'm still uncertain whether we're on the air or not I quickly hand my cell phone to my broadcast partner, George Von Benko, to answer. And, as happens on occasion, George will quickly tell me when we're off the air so that I can quit doing play–by–play that's going nowhere and address the problem.

On December 20th, 2003, Duquesne was hosting George Mason in a four o'clock game at the Palumbo Center, the Dukes' home court. During the second half my cell phone began to vibrate rudely and when I checked the computer screen it appeared we were still on the air, but of course that's not always the case. In any event I promptly handed my phone to George and in between words glanced at George to try to get an indication of what the call was about. After a few seconds he covered his mike and leaned over to me, and when I pulled off my headset mike for a moment I heard him say, "Call your daughter Julie when you get a chance."

Immediately I knew it couldn't be good news. But the game was still going on and I had to force myself to concentrate on the play–by–play, something I usually never have any trouble doing.

I couldn't wait for the next scheduled time–out. Since the media time–outs occur at the first dead ball every four minutes on the clock, the next time–out occurred a few minutes later, even though it seemed like a few hours. When I gave the commercial cue, I quickly accessed my daughter Julie's number, and to my chagrin, the line was busy. I tried again before the time–out expired and again it was busy.

Whatever the news was it couldn't be good, but *how bad could it be*, I thought. If it were absolutely urgent, Julie would have insisted that she talk to me immediately when she spoke to George. I quickly asked George if he knew anything more regarding Julie's conversation. He said, "No. First of all she thought she was talking to you so I had to straighten her out on that, and then she just said to have you call her when you get the chance."

Play resumed and I did my best to concentrate on the play-by-play, but I couldn't help wondering what was going on. Then it hit me. That very morning, Dee and I had taken delivery on her new car, actually a used car, but of course new for her, at Colonial Toyota in Indiana. She had driven it briefly once and had given her approval and after getting the car that morning I headed to Pittsburgh for my broadcast. I knew she had planned to pick up her sister Evelyn, and since it was five days before Christmas they would be finishing their shopping in Indiana.

Now my imagination went to work. *She probably wasn't used to the car yet and was involved in an accident..* I could only hope that she wasn't injured, and that the car was the only thing that was damaged. *That's probably why Julie is calling me. But then why didn't Dee call me? Maybe she was injured.* It's amazing how one's imagination can run wild at times like these.

Meanwhile the game was going on and I kept anxiously waiting for the next time-out so that I could call Julie. Finally there was a time-out and this time Julie answered. First off she didn't realize I was still in the middle of the game. She thought it would be over by now or she wouldn't have called during the game. She quickly told me that Dee and Evelyn were shopping at Sears in the Indiana Mall when Dee either lost her balance or tripped and in trying to brace herself when she fell, had broken her left arm right above the wrist. She had already been to the hospital, where a doctor had set the arm; which was now in a cast. Otherwise she was okay.

I didn't have time to get any other details because the game was about to start again, but at least I knew what was going on. It could have been worse, obviously, much worse.

As soon as the game was over I was able to call Dee and get more details. Fortunately three of our four daughters live in Indiana and they were all with her in a flash, taking better care of her, I'm sure, than I could.

When I finally got to talk to Dee I asked her whether I should come home. Normally I would after a game. But she knew that I intended to stay at our daughter Lisa's home in Monroeville because the next morning the Dukes were flying to Minnesota for a game there on Monday night. Rather than drive back to Indiana after the George Mason game and turn around and drive right back to Pittsburgh early the next day it was much easier to stay with Lisa. Dee insisted she didn't need me to come home and I knew she was being well taken care of, so I really didn't get home to see her with her arm in a cast until Tuesday, three days after the accident.

Several weeks were required before the cast came off and several more weeks of rehab, but Dee recovered nicely from the broken arm.

I still debate with myself whether a cell phone is a good idea. There's the old saying of "no news is good news" and if someone can't get to you immediately with the news I guess that comes under the heading of "no news."

But just like VCR's, microwaves, faxes, computers, CD's and DVD's, cell phones are here to stay, and with reluctance, for better or for worse, I've been dragged into the 21st century of communications.

28

PNC PARK

Can you imagine what a thrill it would be for a high school baseball player to play in a major league ball park?

Well, the Pittsburgh Pirates have a promotional program that allows a limited number of area high schools in western Pennsylvania to do just that.

The school's baseball team sells tickets to future Pirate games. In return the teams which sell the allotted number of tickets get to play at beautiful PNC Park.

On May 3, 2005, Kittanning and West Shamokin High Schools, having sold their quota of tickets, were slated to meet each other at PNC Park at 9:30 a. m.

I was contacted by John DeFeo from WTYM in Kittanning to see whether I was available to tape record the game for re-broadcast later that day. Even though I had to be in Lebanon, Pennsylvania, the day before the game to do a three-hour Invest in Your Debt seminar, something I have done about 20 times a year the past five years at various universities and community colleges through their Continuing Education Departments, I agreed to do the game.

Lebanon is a four-hour drive from Indiana and after the seminar, instead of going home, I drove to my daughter Lisa's home in Monroeville, a Pittsburgh suburb. I figured it would save me an hour's sleep, even though it still amounted to only four and a half-hours of shut-eye.

But there I was at 8:30 a. m. waiting with both teams to enter PNC Park as soon as they opened the gates. As everyone milled around in front of the gate, both coaches, Ed Morris from Kittanning, and Dave Powers with West Shamokin, told me of their teams' efforts to sell the tickets needed to make the game a reality. Both coaches said they had brought everyone who had sold tickets, including their jayvee players, and had promised to get all the players into the game in one capacity or another.

Once the gates opened and we had walked onto the hallowed PNC Park turf, I started to enter all the names, numbers, etc., on my makeshift scorecard. This took some time because first the teams' scorekeepers had to put all that information on the line up cards they use before I could then copy them onto my sheet.

Meanwhile the players started to loosen up, that is, those who didn't have cameras that were already being employed to record this "once in a lifetime" experience.

Then a member of the Pirate staff asked all the members of the West Shamokin team to assemble for some important information. He was very cordial in outlining the "do's and don'ts" of what was expected during warm-ups and the game itself.

There would be no batting practice or "pepper" and it was clear the Pirates were very much concerned about safeguarding their field, especially the grass, which was understandable.

When he was done and had wished the team well, I turned to a player near me and said, "Basically you can do anything you want, just stay off the grass." That was an exaggeration, of course, but not much of one.

Once I had listed all the names of both teams on one page for easy reference, I counted 27 Kittanning players, and noted that West Shamokin had 31. And all of them were going to play. *This should be interesting, if not nightmarish,* I thought.

Both line ups listed ten players as starters. Because high schools are permitted to use designated hitters, I was accustomed to this. After all, if the American League can do it, why not high schools? But instead of the DH initials, I noticed that both teams had an EH listed by the name of their tenth player. Upon questioning, I discovered EH meant extra batter: in other words, each team would bat ten, but only nine would play in the field. You learn something new everyday.

I sat behind home plate to record the game. The West Shamokin and Kittanning fans, numbering in the hundreds and consisting primarily of parents, relatives, and friends of the players, were seated directly behind their teams' respective dugouts along the first- and third-base lines.

The first inning found West Shamokin jumping out to a 2–0 lead. Then the top of the second turned out to be "one for the ages."

Joe Vicini, a slick lefthander, was on the mound for the Wolves of West Shamokin. In his previous outing, he had fanned 15 Freeport hitters in seven innings.

Vicini recorded two K's in the first frame but was to do something in the second inning that very few can brag about.

A Wolves' error put the Wildcats' Jeremy DeLuca on base and after he stole second, Jared Bowser struck out on a pitch in the dirt that catcher Nate Hayes had trouble coming up with, and when he finally did, he threw wild to first base enabling DeLuca to score.

Vicini proceeded to strike out the next two batters, meaning that he already had three strikeouts in the inning and a chance to get a "once in a lifetime" four K's in one inning.

Bowser, after first stealing second, proceeded to steal third. When Vicini walked Tim Brocious, who promptly stole second, Vicini went to a full windup with second and third occupied.

On a two and two pitch to right-handed batter Brian Arble, Bowser broke for home. Vicini, being left-handed, never saw him coming down the line. His pitch to the plate arrived as Bowser was beginning his slide home. Arble took the pitch. Catcher Nate Hayes couldn't receive the ball fast enough to tag the sliding Bowser, but home plate umpire Jimmy Smith called the pitch strike three, making it the side-retiring out, disallowing the apparent steal of home by Bowser, and giving Vicini an incredible four-strikeout inning!

West Shamokin scored another run in the bottom of the second to take a 3–1 lead, and when Kittanning came to bat in the top of the third, the lead-off hitter was none other than Brian Arble, the same Brian Arble who had been called out on strikes to end the top of the second.

This threw me into a quandary. I wondered what I had possibly missed. How could Arble have struck out to end one inning and then lead off the next? Did Hayes actually tag Bowser as he slid home for the third out? That would explain why Arble was leading off. But no, I was certain home plate umpire Jimmy Smith had raised his right arm to indicate a third strike and that ended the inning.

I speculated on these possibilities as Arble began his at-bat in the third inning. And, wouldn't you know it, Arble struck out again to lead off the third inning.

During the half-inning break, I sought clarification from a couple of scouts seated several rows in front of me as to exactly what did happen in that second inning. They confirmed that indeed the batter had been called out on strikes to end the inning.

As the game progressed I began to realize that maybe, just maybe, I was the only person actually "trying" to keep score. I say "trying" because, as promised, both coaches started substituting liberally, in that third inning.

There were pinch runners, pinch batters, defensive changes, new pitchers, virtually every inning, thus presenting quite a challenge to anyone trying to keep up with the revolving cast of players. And of course since re-entry was permitted, players who were once in the game could come back, and as I soon discovered they didn't even have to bat in their original spot, not to mention play a different position. "Anything goes" would be an understatement to describe the goings-on.

Since the game would be re-broadcast at four that afternoon, I knew the parents and relatives watching the game would also be home in time to listen to the replay, so I really concentrated on trying to identify every player who came into the game.

At one point, Kittanning had five jayvee and four varsity players on the field. I knew that because the jayvees had different uniforms of a different color, which was fine.

But West Shamokin's jayvee players had the same uniforms as the varsity and some even had the same numbers. In the sixth inning, Tyler Cloak, a jayvee pitcher wearing number 15, took the mound for the Wolves. Kittanning scored once to cut West Shamokin's lead to 8-6. When the Wolves failed to score in the bottom of the sixth, the Wildcats had their last chance as Number 15 headed for the mound.

But Kittanning's first batter went down swinging as Number 15 seemed to find a little more zip on his fastball. Then I realized the West Shamokin fans were exhorting their pitcher to close things out by shouting, "Come on Jake." *Whoa*, I thought, *the Number 15 on the hill was the varsity 15 Jacob Houser. No wonder he looked faster.* I quickly made the correction as Houser got another strikeout and a fly ball to right field to end the game, giving West Shamokin the win 8–6.

As I drove away from PNC Park heading for Kittanning to drop off the tape for later broadcast, I thought, *Well, at least I mentioned all 58 players who played at least once, and I'll never forget that "once in a lifetime" second inning that featured four strikeouts and a steal of home that was disallowed by that final record–tying strikeout.*

29

TWO-TIME SURVIVOR

As I write this I have been broadcasting Duquesne basketball on the radio for 40 consecutive years. Twice I came close, very close to having that streak broken, once my fourth year, and the second time in year 21.

WJAS in Pittsburgh was the first station to carry the games in 1968 when I originally began announcing them. Earl Buncher was the General Manager of WJAS, an NBC owned and operated station that was all news and talk at the time. So sports fit in with that type of format, and Buncher was the person who hired me, with Duquesne's blessing.

After three seasons WJAS was sold and the new owner, Cecil Heftel, changed the format to rock music and Duquesne basketball was looking for a new radio home. Buncher, meanwhile, had moved on to become a partner in the Louis Sautel Advertising Agency in Pittsburgh. And Earl along with the Sautel Agency became the producers of Duquesne basketball, with Duquesne's approval of course. That meant Earl was responsible for finding a station to carry the games, sell the advertising, assume the responsibility for all the bills, including paying the talent, all the expenses, and try to make a profit for his agency.

Since I had gotten to know Earl over the three years I did the games for WJAS, he was my boss then and continued to be my boss. We had an excellent relationship and I have always valued what Earl did for me.

KDKA, the nation's first radio station, and the 50,000 watt powerhouse in Pittsburgh expressed interest in carrying the Duquesne games, and Earl was able to negotiate with them to get them on the air. And he proposed that since I had been doing the games that I should continue as the voice of the Dukes.

But it wasn't as easy as that, because at precisely the same time KDKA became the Dukes' station, Bill Currie became the Sports Director of KDKA-TV. Currie came to Pittsburgh from North Carolina, where he had been the longtime voice of North Carolina basketball in addition to his TV sports work. He had a big reputation. In fact, *Sports Illustrated* wrote a feature article on him, dubbing him "The Mouth of the South." And when he found out that KDKA would be carrying the Duquesne games, he was interested in doing the play–by–play. I knew KDKA had a lot of clout so I really thought I would be on the outside looking in.

But thanks to Earl Buncher and Duquesne, it was proposed to KDKA that Currie and I both do the games, in other words split the play–by–play. Apparently Currie didn't want to share the play–by–play duties and decided doing the sports on TV was enough. So I survived, barely, thanks to Earl Buncher, Duquesne, and frankly, Bill Currie.

After Pittsburgh's most powerful station, KDKA, had carried the Dukes for one year, it decided not to renew and Earl Buncher had to look for another station. Over the course of the next 16 years the games were heard on KQV, WWSW, WJAS, and back to KQV again. Fortunately because of my relationship with Buncher and Duquesne I continued to broadcast the games each year.

Meanwhile at one point Buncher left Pittsbugh for the west coast and other employment. The Sautel Agency continued to maintain the rights. After a couple of years Buncher returned and actually took over complete production of the games by himself through his firm Action Communications.

Then in 1989, a big change occurred at Duquesne University when Brian Colleary was named Athletic Director. The Dukes had suffered seven losing seasons in the past eight and Buncher was having trouble getting enough advertisers to pay the freight to keep the Dukes on the air.

Colleary, who had come from Marist College in Poughkeepsie, New York, wanted Duquesne University to produce the games, and Buncher was in no position to argue and really was about to pull the plug anyhow.

A meeting was held with Buncher, Colleary, and myself, and Earl outlined what had transpired in the past and said to Brian he would do anything he could to be helpful in the transition period.

I didn't like the fact that Buncher wouldn't be involved anymore but there wasn't anything I could do. Not only did Earl always pay me promptly but he would give me money up-front on expenses after which I would account for my lodging and meals, etc., and we never had any problems.

But change is the only thing that is constant, and Duquesne became my new boss or at least I thought it had.

Colleary hired a new coach in John Carroll and was very busy settling into his new job. It was nearly a month before the first scheduled game and as I hadn't heard a word I called him just to confirm that everything would remain the same as far as the broadcasts were concerned.

There are certain moments in everyone's life where you remember exactly where you were and what was said, and the phone call with Brian Colleary was one of those moments in my life.

I was sitting on our steps that head up to our bedrooms talking to Brian when I heard him say, "Well I've been thinking about making a change with regard to the radio broadcasts."

"Change, what do you mean change, Brian?" I responded.

"Well, I've been doing some checking around. And it seems that no one really knows who you are. I mean Pitt has Bill Hillgrove doing their games and he's on TV so that gives Pitt basketball a higher profile. I'm thinking we need someone who can help us promote Duquesne basketball better beyond just doing the games," Brian went on.

I was quick to reply. "Well Brian, as you know the Dukes have had several losing seasons, attendance is down, and naturally people are not as interested in Duquesne basketball as they were when I started doing the games in '68 and they were big winners and I had articles written about me and my play-by-play ability."

"Well, I haven't made up my mind yet. In fact, I'm thinking that I might go with two broadcast crews, one for home games and one for road games, and if I do, and you're one of the play-by-play men, I would hope you would do the road games because obviously there would be more listeners. It's something I'm kicking around," Brian said.

I thought *well that's interesting. No one knows me and now I'm looking at doing half the games. That should guarantee that more people will know me.*

I quickly responded. "Brian," I said, "I think we need to sit down face to face and discuss this and I'm wondering if you have some time," (and I gave him two dates and times just as my previous sales training had taught me) and we agreed on a time to meet.

Driving to Pittsburgh for the meeting, I thought *well, Ray, half a loaf is better than none,* as I prepared to meet with Brian.

I began the meeting by saying "Brian, you're the boss, and whatever you decide after we meet I want you to know I will not criticize you or say anything that would hurt Duquesne basketball."

We then discussed the pros and cons of two announcers rather than one, and frankly why perhaps someone else could do a better job of promoting the games. I could see Brian's objection to me wasn't personal. He just wanted someone with a bigger name, someone who to his way of thinking would help the Duquesne program.

When I left, we shook hands, and he said he would make up his mind soon and let me know what he decided. At that point I thought I'm either doing half the games or none. This was three weeks before the first game.

Several days passed without any word, except for an item that appeared in the *Pittsburgh Post-Gazette* as reported by Phil Axelrod, who covered the Dukes for the PG. I didn't know Phil's source, but he had it right. The item indicated that Ray Goss might just be doing half of the Dukes games, if that.

The Dukes played two pre-season games before the regular season started and I always attended them even though they weren't broadcast on the radio. I needed to get as familiar with the team as possible. It was halftime of the first pre season game after the item hit the papers when I was approached by a woman I had never met. She introduced herself as Mary Ann Pflumm, and said she has been following the Dukes for years and listened to my broadcasts.

"I have one question for you, Ray," Mary Ann began, "Is it your idea to cut back and do only half the games?"

"No," I smiled, "you know there have been some changes here at Duquesne and this is the new athletic director's idea."

"That's what I thought," she said, "Well, we'll see, I intend to do something if you don't mind?"

"Not at all," I said, "I don't think you can hurt my chances."

With that Mary Ann left and I had no idea what she was about to do, but I soon

MARY ANN PFLUMM
I refer to Mary Ann as the president (and only member) of my fan club. She was determined that I not lose my Duquesne play–by–play job and I can never thank her enough for her efforts on my behalf.

found out. Mary Ann knows how to write a persuasive letter and she did exactly that, to the President of Duquesne, Dr. John Murray. Not only that, she persuaded other Duquesne fans who were season ticket holders to do the same.

Ten days before the first game I still hadn't heard a word from Brian Colleary. I did hear from Goose Goslin, the Sports Director for KDKA Radio, who called me one morning to inquire about the Duquesne situation.

Goose had attended IUP and as a student worked part–time for me at WDAD when I was the manager. Later when he landed a job in Pittsburgh he did the color commentary for me on the Duquesne broadcasts for a couple of years. Now he was working with John Cigna, the morning man at KDKA, who also had worked with me on the Duquesne broadcasts when he was at WJAS.

Goose said that he and John had been talking about Duquesne and John, never shy about sounding off, wanted to say something on his morning show about why they would even consider getting rid of me or allowing me to do only half the games. Goose told John he wanted to check with me to see if it was all right. I told Goose I didn't think they could hurt my cause.

The next morning, November 22nd, one week before the Dukes' first game, and following one of Goose's sports reports, John asked Goose on the air, "What is the story on Ray Goss and Duquesne basketball?" John said he was "getting on his soap box" and proceeded in his inimitable style to question the possible decision by Duquesne to "dump Ray Goss."

At the conclusion of the brief dialogue, Goose and John urged their listeners to call the Duquesne President John Murray if they felt the same as they did.

I didn't know whether anything would come of this, but I certainly appreciated John and Goose's support.

On Saturday, November 25th, IUP was scheduled to play Portland State in Portland, Oregon, in the NCAA Division II football play-offs and Jack Benedict and I flew from Pittsburgh to Portland on the Friday before the game for our broadcast on 1160 WCCS.

Following the game we caught the "red eye" and landed in Pittsburgh early Sunday morning, November 26th, three days before the Dukes' first game. Coincidentally IUP's basketball season was set to begin on the same day, Wednesday, November 29th.

As we waited at the airport for our luggage I said to Jack, "I'm going to buy the Sunday *Pittsburgh Press*. Maybe there's something in there that will tell me whether I'm doing the Duquesne game Wednesday or whether I'll be working with you doing the IUP game."

When I flipped to the sports pages of the *Press* I noticed a small item that said Ray Goss would be doing the broadcasts of the Dukes' games once again with former head coach John Cinicola doing the color on the home games and George Von Benko the road games.

I remember saying casually to Jack, "Well it looks like I'll be doing the Duquesne games, at least that's what it says here in the paper."

The next morning I got a call from Mary Ann Pflumm. She was excited, saying how she read about the fact I'd be doing all the games. I recall saying to her, "I guess so. I saw the same item in the paper."

She said, "You mean no one from Duquesne called you?"

I said, "No, but remember I've been out of town for the past couple of days and it was Thanksgiving weekend."

She said, "Well I'm going to call Duquesne right now to make sure and I'll get right back to you."

Not five minutes later Mary Ann called to confirm that indeed I'd be doing the games. And that's how I found out that I'd been rehired, first by reading it in the newspaper and then by having it confirmed by Mary Ann Pflumm. Since that day, I have always referred to Mary Ann as the president of my fan club.

I don't know what would have happened if it weren't for Mary Ann's efforts, and from what I understand several calls to President Murray's office following the comments by John Cigna and Goose Goslin.

But I had survived for the second time, this one going into my 22nd year of broadcasting the Dukes' games, and I haven't had any close calls since, knock on wood.

30

POTPOURRI

In compiling notes for this book, I wound up with a "potpourri" of incidents that have occurred over the years and still stand out in my mind. At the time they happened some of them were anything but pleasant, but now, given the advantage of time, I can look back on them with amusement.

One of the biggest problems I've had to cope with in broadcasting football games is the public address system. Notice I said system, not public address announcers, although there are a fair number of them who attempt to do a radio play-by-play of the action instead of simply identifying the ball carrier, the tackler, the yards gained or lost and what down it is and how much yardage is needed for a first down.

The problem is that I've never heard a P. A. system that wasn't loud enough. On the contrary, most of them can be heard miles away. Now when you're broadcasting a game, and it just so happens one of the speakers is near your broadcast position, guess what? Right, it sounds like the P. A. announcer is doing the game on the radio, not you.

The worst case I ever ran into occurred in a game in Clarion, Pa., between Clarion State College and Indiana State College. At this particular game, Paul McGregor, a good friend and Indiana fan, was accompanying me. Because I was doing the radio broadcast by myself, Paul said he would keep the basic statistics.

When we arrived at the game site, we were told that our broadcast position would be on top of the small press box. That was fine with me because the press box was jammed and it was a nice fall day. We weren't concerned about inclement weather.

We made our way up the ladder onto the roof, where we were given a table and two chairs. I set up our equipment and ran an extension cord to the booth below, where it was plugged into a power outlet.

When, just prior to the start of the game, the P. A. announcer ran down the starting line ups, I knew we were in trouble. The two speakers for the P. A. system were positioned on each corner of the roof and the decibel level had to be off the charts. I could see the volume meter on our equipment peaking to the maximum and that was confirmed by what I was hearing in my headsets. There was no way anyone would hear my description of the game while the P. A. announcer was speaking.

After going down the ladder, I politely asked the P. A. announcer whether he could lower the volume, to which he replied, "There's no way I can do that, because the volume is preset." That didn't make any sense to me, but I was in no position to argue with him.

I quickly ascended the ladder and discussed my dilemma with Paul, who came up with an idea.

"Ray," he said, "as loud as this P. A. system is, they'll never know that we disconnected one of the speakers."

"Do you think you can do that, Paul?" I asked.

"No problem. Just give me a screwdriver."

In no time at all Paul had the speaker to our right disconnected. I repositioned our table on the extreme right on the press box roof, as far away as possible from the speaker on the left.

That was much better and no one at the game site ever suspected what we had done. To this day I can't remember whether Paul reconnected that speaker before we left or not.

Then there was the time I was broadcasting a volleyball match from Shippensburg, Pa. This was for the girls' state championship, and John DeFeo from WTYM in Kittanning had made the arrangements with the people at Shippensburg University.

Tony Bernardi, the Athletic Director at Shannock Valley, the team we were following, was my broadcast partner. Because Tony knew a whole lot more about volleyball than I did, I was mighty glad to have him along.

I had gotten to know Tony over the years as he was very active in

TONY BERNARDI

An excellent basketball coach whose speciality was teaching and coaching defense. You can see how much Head Coach Carl Davis (on the right) and Assistant Tom Beck (on the left) had for Tony because he's right in the middle of the IUP huddle telling the team what to do on defense.

the basketball coaching ranks and I could recall when he played point guard for Geneva College, who tangled with Duquesne University back in the '50s when I was a student at Duquesne.

Tony was a very successful high school coach who moved on to be a top-flight assistant at IUP. His expertise was in teaching defense and Carl Davis, then Tom Beck, the coaches at IUP in the '70s credited Tony with much of IUP's success.

The first match of the weekend volleyball tournament was slated for 9:30 Friday morning. Because it was so early, the doors to the gym were not opened until nine a. m. Fortunately at 8:45 we were able to gain access to the gym in order to set up our equipment and check out the line ups.

Since we were doing the game on a cell phone we looked for a power outlet to connect the cell phone and found one on the wall above the last row of stands. As the match began, everything seemed fine, and all went well until midway through the first set. I had just called for a commercial break when a man approached our broadcast position, exclaiming in some heat, "Hang up that phone right now."

I thought I heard what he said but I did have my headsets on and couldn't believe my ears. "What?" I asked incredulously.

"You heard me. Hang up that phone right now. You do not have permission to broadcast this match," was his angry reply.

After a brief discussion I was made aware that even though arrangements had been made with Shippensburg, no one had called the Pennsylvania Interscholastic Athletic Association to request permission to broadcast the matches.

I promptly apologized to the gentleman, asking politely what we might do to resolve the matter.

"Well," he said, "there's the matter of a $50 rights fee that needs to be paid,"

On hearing this, Tony quickly opened his wallet, produced $50, and handed it to the PIAA official. Disaster had been averted.

As he was leaving and we were allowed to continue the broadcast, I had one departing comment for the PIAA official. "We'll need a receipt for that $50," I said. We really didn't need the receipt. I knew the radio station would reimburse Tony the money. I guess I just felt I needed to get in the last word.

Radio Station WTYM in Kittanning, Pa. originates more sports play-by-play events than any other station I've ever known. During high school football season it's not uncommon for it to have five or six games on the weekend. Since only two of these games are normally broadcast live, one on Friday night and another on Saturday afternoon or evening, the others need to be tape recorded for later broadcast.

I was tape recording one of these games in Apollo, Pa., on a Friday night. The first half went fine, and after I did a quick wrap-up of the first half, I flipped the tape over to record the second half of the game. I thought everything had gone all right with the second half also, that is until I began driving home and put the tape into my car's tape deck just to make sure. After spot checking the first-half action, I turned the tape over to check the second half and heard absolutely nothing. I fast forwarded the tape. Still nothing. I rewound it and hit "play" again. Nothing. I pulled the car to the side of the road and switched on the light in the car as I ejected the tape to look at it. The tape hadn't got twisted, which I was hoping was the case, because then I would simply straighten out the tape and in all likelihood everything would be okay. I was at a loss to explain why there was nothing on side two of the tape. I remembered seeing the red light on the meter being lit while I was recording. Next I reached for my tape recorder to examine it. I inserted the tape and that's when I noticed there was a problem with the lid. It didn't always fit precisely when the tape was inserted. That would mean the tape wasn't positioned properly and even though it looked as if it were recording, it wasn't. Reality set in. Side two was blank. The question now was *what do I do?*

As I began driving back home I pondered my options. Do I just explain what happened and give a summary of the second-half scores? Or, do I try to re-create the second half of action? After all, I had pretty good notes, and I could try to fill in the rest. As I approached Indiana, I made up my mind. I pulled into a nearly empty shopping center parking lot. It was 10:45 p. m. I put on the interior light in the car, arranged my notes, inserted the tape into the recorder and, by testing it, made sure it was recording. Then I re-created the whole second half. Of course since I didn't have the result of every play recorded in my notes, I had to fabricate more than a few plays. But I knew when every touchdown was scored. The one thing I couldn't manage was to re-create the crowd noise. Oh well, you can't have everything.

After about 20 minutes of work, much shorter than the second half would actually take, I wrapped up the game, not forgetting to include statistics.

To this day I think I made the right decision. I don't even feel guilty about not admitting on tape what I was doing. You've heard of "literary license," haven't you? I guess re-creating could be listed under the category of "audio allowance."

31

"JUST THEIR HOME GAMES"

One of the most amusing incidents that ever occurred during my radio career did not happen while I was on the air. It had nothing at all to do with the actual broadcast account of the game.

In the fall of 1960, in the very good company of Joe Termin, who was manager of the WDAD radio station in Indiana, and Paul McGregor, a dear friend and football fan, I drove on the scheduled Saturday to Lock Haven in order to broadcast the conference football game between the State Teachers Colleges Lock Haven and Indiana. All of us knew well enough how to get to Clearfield and follow the West Branch of the Susquehanna River east to the community of Lock Haven; but none of us had ever been to the college campus, and of course we had no idea in the world where the football stadium might be located. Consequently, we left Indiana in plenty of time.

As we drove into the community at about eleven o'clock in the morning, a full two and a half-hours before game time, and began to follow signs which directed strangers to the campus of "Lock Haven State Teachers College," we perceived (near the river) a stadium and what, to our trained eyes, was clearly a football field.

"This must be where the game is to be played," observed Joe, whose logic Paul and I regularly found astonishing.

"It sure looks like it," I offered politely, "but we'd better check it out."

At this hour we had no difficulty in parking our automobile. As we strolled into the empty stadium, I headed for what appeared to be the press box. Finding the door locked, I peered through the window to see whether I might be able to spot a radio hook-up labeled WDAD. Unfortunately, I could not see anything of that kind. I was left to wonder whether we had the college stadium, or perhaps a high school field.

Then, as I looked clear through the press box to the field below, I noticed that we were not altogether alone in this stadium. Far down below, an elderly man was plodding along behind a grotesque machine, hoping apparently to produce with white lime some lines so well ordered as to regulate the playing surface.

When I reported this discovery to the others, Joe exclaimed that "There must be a game here today."

That was good news for Paul and me. But of course I had to know just whose game it was. So I yelled down to the worker, with my radio voice, "Excuse me, sir, but is this where Lock Haven State Teachers College plays its football games?"

Startled, the man tripped a device on his limer, turned from his machine to peer up at us, paused for a moment, then replied, "Well, not all of their games, just their home games."

Okay, I mused, as I did everything possible to suppress my laughter. I noted that Joe and Paul were reacting likewise.

I did manage to blurt out a "Thank you," and we happily made our exit from the Lock Haven State Teachers College Stadium, and headed for a restaurant, which we felt confident we could locate.

Ten minutes later we were at lunch, and still laughing, as we took turns repeating the obvious but precisely correct words we had just heard from the man liming the football field, "Well, not all their games, just their home games."

32

OPENING DAY

John DeFeo, the ace salesman for Radio Station WTYM in Kittanning, called me in late April of 2004. He wanted to know whether I could broadcast the opening-day game of the Shannock Valley Little League in Rural Valley on Saturday, May 1st.

"It starts at 10 a. m.," John said, "so you won't even tie up your whole Saturday." John was selling me just as he sold many clients on so many different sporting events for the Kittanning station. He did that so often that I once told him, "John, you could sell ice water to Eskimos."

But I told John I could do the game and when I asked him about information on the two teams who would be playing he said he had nothing, but promised me that if I got there early, someone from the Shannock Valley Little League would have information for me.

Well, it wasn't ideal, but what could I expect? After all, it was Little League, not the majors. And they pay me the same rate for a Little League game that I get for a high school basketball play-off contest. So, at 8:15 on Saturday morning, May 1st, I headed to the Shannock Valley Little League Field, only a half-hour drive from my home in Indiana.

At 8:45 I arrived to find various volunteers getting the field in shape and organizing the concession stand. I located my contact person, who began by saying "You are doing all four games today, aren't you?"

"Uh, no, that's not my understanding?"

"Well, last year on opening day, your station did all four games."

"I don't know anything about last year, but I was told by John DeFeo that we were doing only the first game. I'll tell you what. I'll call him at home now and we'll get this straightened out."

There was no way I wanted to do four games. One of the reasons I had accepted the job was because of the 10 o'clock start, and I had promised Dee I'd be back and we would go out shopping in the afternoon and then have dinner afterwards.

Well, as luck would have it, my cell phone was in a no-service area and I couldn't get John. One of the lady volunteers offered me her phone to try, but said, "We're in a dead spot here and usually no one's cell phone works, but you're welcome to try mine."

She was right, nothing.

I decided to be a little more aggressive.

"I don't want to cause any problems, but I know John told me we'd be carrying the first game today. He never mentioned four games because there's no way I can stay and do all four games."

"Okay," came the quick reply. And amazingly that problem was settled.

Now I had to get the line ups for the first game.

"Who's playing in the first game?" I asked cheerfully.

"Well our first game is the Minor League game between Klings and Spaces Corners," I was told.

"You mean eight- and nine-year olds?" I asked.

"Well, there are some ten-year olds too."

"Okay, fine," I said. "Who has the line ups?"

I was directed to the manager of the Klings team, and after I got the names and ages of his players, (ten of them, for they had a rover), I sought out the Spaces Corners' manager. It turns out they had only nine players; they would play without a rover.

Then the two managers met and luckily I hung around for the meeting.

One of them said, "Are we going to let the kids pitch or are we going to pitch?"

After a discussion they agreed that since this was the first game perhaps the managers should pitch and there would be a seven-pitch limit to each batter with no walks.

Good, I thought. I could just imagine how many walks there would be with an eight- or nine-year-old pitching on opening day.

There were other rules the two managers discussed and agreed on, the likes of which I had never heard before but of course needed to know if I was going to broadcast this game and know what was going on.

The limit for each at-bat would occur when the side batted around. I liked that rule too.

"What about balls hit in the outfield that go through someone's legs?" one of the managers asked the other.

"What do you mean?"

"Well the minor league rules we adopted last year said that a ball that goes through an outfielder's legs is two bases, but balls hit between the fielders it's all you can get," said the first manager. After a discussion of this perplexing situation they agreed that it would be all you can get on anything hit to the outfield.

Good again, I thought.

Finally the game was ready to begin, and I had my card table and tape recorder set up just outside the fence along the third-base line not far from my car. I like taping games for later broadcast because I can pause the tape when there are delays and that makes my job a lot easier.

The first couple of innings went by rather quickly. The seven-pitch limit with no walks really helped. Then in the top of the third inning the third out was recorded, and I dutifully reported, "That's out number three, and with the score Klings six, Spaces Corners three we'll move to the bottom of the third inning right after this break on AM 1380 WTYM."

I paused the tape, but instead of the teams changing sides another batter moved into the box and the manager was all set to toss him the first pitch. I reacted quickly, "There are three outs," I said loud enough for everyone on the field to hear. The manager-pitcher on the field hesitated, paused, and then realized that indeed there were three outs and the teams changed sides.

A half-inning later big rain drops started descending, not enough to stop play, but certainly enough to create havoc with my spotting sheet and scorecard. After the first out, I paused the tape, and high-tailed it to my car nearby, keeping one eye on the field in case something important happened. I opened my trunk and grabbed an umbrella and didn't miss more than three or four pitches.

In the fourth inning after one team batted around, meaning the inning was over, I dutifully reported the score as Klings 12, Spaces Corners 3. When I paused the tape I checked the scoreboard, which had the score 9 to 3, not 12 to 3. I checked my scorebook again, and counted all the runs that had scored and sure enough the score should have been 12 to 3. Eventually the score was changed to 11 to 3 and since that was the official score I had to go with it.

When the top of the fifth inning ended, I went to break by announcing that "The bottom of the fifth inning comes up right after this break on AM 1380 WTYM." I paused the tape and watched in disbelief as the players lined up and began to shake hands, indicating that the game was over at the end of four and a half innings. Why, I have no idea, except possibly there was also a time limit which I was not aware of. So I had to come back on, wipe the egg off my face, and report that the game was over with the final score being 11 to 3, even though it was actually 12 to 3.

All I could do was smile to myself and think, *Well, Ray, this has definitely been a first, the first time I didn't know a game was over when it was over.*

As I drove away from the ball field to deliver the audio tape to the Kittanning radio station, I couldn't help but relive some of the improbable events that I had just witnessed and thought, *Well, at least today's game will make a chapter in the book I'll write someday.*

33

CLICHES AND PET PEEVES

Occasionally a broadcaster will create a catchy phrase and before you can say "Jack Robinson" others pick it up and it then becomes part of the sports lexicon.

One that's in vogue now and has been for a couple of years is "Put the ball on the floor." I wish I had a nickel for every time I've hear that expression used by radio and TV basketball announcers. In fact, I don't recall watching or listening to a game during the last decade when I haven't heard it.

So why do I object to the use of "Put the ball on the floor?" Well, in the wonderful game of basketball there's one word that effectively replaces those six words and does it beautifully. And that word is "DRIBBLE." It's a basketball term that has been around as long as basketball itself since bouncing the ball is an inherent part of the game. But someone, somewhere, decided to use "Put the ball on the floor." Then someone else used it, and then someone else, and now it has grown to epidemic proportions. I guess the word "dribble" seems old fashioned to the current crop of sports announcers.

I suppose what the "Put the ball on the floor" practitioners are really trying to convey to their audience is the fact that the person "who puts the ball on the floor" is more adept at dribbling than someone who merely dribbles the ball. Maybe if I'm lucky, by the time you've read this, "Put the ball on the floor" will have gone out of style and another term, maybe even "dribble," will have replaced it. Don't bet on it.

In the same venue is the term "Put points on the board," as in "Team A really needs to put some points on the board." How about the word "SCORE" instead of "put points on the board?" Is not the meaning the same? Again, perhaps the broadcaster is trying to stress the fact that Team A hasn't "put any points on the board" for a while, and really needs to do that posthaste in order to get into the game.

Which brings me to my favorite. When the ten foul rule came into being, a move that was intended to discourage fouling at the end of the game in order to cut down on the time it was taking to play the last minute or two, someone said Team A is now in the "double bonus." By the way, the ten foul rule has not discouraged fouling in the least. And now everyone, there are no exceptions that I recall save one (guess who?), uses the term "double bonus" when one team commits its tenth foul of the half.

Let's examine the term "double bonus."

By definition, bonus means an addition. So "double bonus" would logically mean twice in addition. But to get a bonus you must have something first that could be added to, in this case a free-throw. So you have one free throw and when you get a bonus that means you have two free throws. And when you get a "double bonus," doesn't it follow that you get three free throws?

But you don't get three. What you get are a guaranteed two free throws, as opposed to the "one and one" when a seventh team foul is committed. Of course with the "one and one" you must make the first before you get the second, so it really isn't a bonus because it's not guaranteed, whereas the so-called "double bonus" guarantees you two shots. That to me is a weak argument for the term "double bonus." Why not something simple, like two shots? So when Team A commits its 10th foul, Team B simply gets two shots.

By the way, when I bring this up with other broadcasters, in addition to getting strange looks the usual retort is "Well, that's what everyone calls it." Okay, but I prefer to call it two shots. Now you know the one person referred to above who doesn't use the term "double bonus."

As long as I'm on my soapbox, there's one rule in basketball that I would definitely change if I were the "Basketball Rules Czar" with unlimited power. I would not allow a player or coach to call a time-out just because his player is about to commit a turnover.

One example. The ball is going out of bounds and the player while airborne snags the ball and before he lands calls a time-out.

And the referee dutifully signals time-out and the announcer hails the brilliant reaction of the player.

Since I wrote this, the rule was changed in college ball. A player heading out of bounds with the ball cannot call a time-out. Congratulations Rules Committee.

Here's another example. Team A is pressing Team B. A player from Team A is trapped by two defenders and can't find an outlet. He's in jeopardy of having the five-second close guarding rule called against him; so he calls a time-out. A similar situation occurs on a scramble for a loose ball when a player from Team A comes up with the ball on the floor and a player from Team B is ready to tie him up. "Time out" the player from Team A yells; and his team is awarded the time-out.

I can just hear the arguments against implementing this rule. It will make it too difficult for the officials to determine when a player is in jeopardy of calling a time-out. Horsefeathers. Everyone in the arena knows that when one of the above situations occurs the only reason a time-out is sought is to avoid a turnover or a held ball.

To me it smacks of a get out of jail free card in Monopoly. Team B double-teams a player from Team A. They're ready to force an errant pass or a five-second violation and for their reward they get to see Team A call a time-out.

Maybe just one more rule change as "Czar."

I was in favor of the shot clock when it came into college basketball. But do you remember it was 45 seconds when it was introduced? The women's game has been 30 seconds for some time. Fortunately it didn't take long for the men's college game to shorten the clock to 35 seconds. Better, but why not 30 seconds as it is in the women's game? That's plenty of time and here's the kicker. When the shot clock is shortened to 30 seconds, eliminate the five-second guarding rule. That will help the officials and it's a very subjective call in my estimation. I think the officials would like this one. Some coaches may not, but I feel certain the players would and after all it is supposed to a players' game, isn't it?

In my estimation basketball is the ultimate team game and my favorite team sport. The changes I have witnessed over the years including the shot clock and the three-point shot have, in my opinion, made a great game even better. But the game of basketball can be improved and maybe, just maybe, some of my suggested tweaking of the rules, if enacted, would make basketball an even better game than it is today.

34

BOWLING,
HARNESS RACING, VOLLEYBALL,
AND OUTHOUSE RACES

Over the years as I did more play-by-play sports on the radio in Indiana, Pa., primarily basketball, football, and baseball, more opportunities to broadcast other sports came my way.

And being the adventurous type, at least when I was much younger, I figured I could learn the basics of other sports and broadcast them too.

In the early 1960s, a bowling war developed in Indiana. Calderone's had been the only local bowling alley until two others opened within months of each other, Ridge Lanes and Indian Lanes.

Since Calderone's had all the leagues and regular bowlers, both Ridge and Indian Lanes became very promotional. You could bowl for as little as 25 cents a line at either place as both new bowling establishments competed for the Indiana County bowlers.

Then, Indian lanes came up with an idea to get the established bowlers into their building and approached WDAD with a proposal to hold a tournament that would be broadcast on the radio.

That's when I began calling bowling on the radio on Sundays from Indian Lanes. The tournament, replete with cash prizes, was able to attract nearly all of the top local bowlers.

Because I've bowled a little myself, I knew terms like "strike," "spare," the "7-10 split," etc. So it wasn't very difficult to describe the action. Example: "Wagner, with a three-step approach, sends his ball down the lane... it hooks into the pocket and, ooh, he leaves the seven pin."

I would talk to the bowlers after each frame live on the radio, getting their instant reaction on what had happened on their most recent effort, and that's how bowling was broadcast on the radio, a first for Indiana, Pa.

Harness racing was much more difficult for me to broadcast. First off, at the time I got into it, I had never seen a harness race and thus wasn't familiar with the terminology of the sport. I literally had to have "my arm twisted" to become involved in calling the races, which by the way weren't on the radio, but on the P.A. System at the Indiana County Fair.

Here's how it happened.

Because I did the public address announcing at the Indiana County Fair, I spent most of the week on the fair grounds. One year, I was approached by Harness Race Secretary Les Serian. It seems the man who had announced the races for years was no longer available, and Les wanted me to call the races.

"No way," I told Les. I knew nothing about harness racing. I didn't follow the sport and didn't even know how to go about describing the races.

But Les was persistent. "You announce other sports and have a good voice, Ray, and we'll be right there to help you."

When I finally agreed to give it a try, I plunged into research. I learned quickly that harness horses don't run, but race, pace, or trot. When they "run" they've broken stride and have to get back on gait.

Identifying the horses was difficult because anywhere from five to eight horses would be entered in each race. The horses' numbers were difficult to see at times, even with binoculars, especially when they were three and four wide rounding a turn or heading down the stretch.

I quickly discovered that seeing the colors the drivers wore was much easier. The only problem there was that if there were seven horses in a race there might be three drivers with green and red silks, and two with blue and white.

That's when I began taking one of my children's crayons to the races, and actually picking out the correct colors to coincide with the drivers' silks. Later I discovered it was easier just to write blue and white, for example, right next to the horse's number, instead of using a blue-and-white crayon. This made it a bit easier to identify the horses rather than trying to see the numbers on the saddle pads, which could be obscured much of the time.

I've continued to call the harness races at both the Indiana County and Dayton, Pa. Fairs for over 30 years now. I recall that during the first year I called the races in Indiana someone had left a gate open in the backstretch and one of the horses going down the backstretch went right through the opening and wound up trotting down Carter Avenue adjacent to the race track. Cars had to pull off left and right in order to avoid the runaway horse. I did my best to describe not only the actual race but the fact that a horse was running its own race down a heavily traveled city street. I can't recall whether the horse was on stride or not.

What a way to break in as an announcer for a new sport!

In 1997, John DeFeo from WTYM in Kittanning called to ask me to do the Shannock Valley girls volleyball matches from Shippensburg, Pa., as they attempted to win the state championship.

"John," I said, "here's what I know about volleyball, you're allowed to hit the ball three times and you have to win a game by two points."

But John was persistent and after all I was available and it would mean some extra money that I could always use.

Long story short, I attended a Shannock Valley practice and met Coach Mark Risko who patiently explained some of the basic rules.

West Shamokin Athletic Director Tony Bernardi, a long-time friend who coached basketball for years, did the "color" commentary on the broadcasts. Tony knew the sport, the officials' signals, and could analyze strategy. He really helped me learn not only the basics of the sport, but also the strategies.

When West Shamokin won the state title, the positive comments we received on the radio broadcasts were very gratifying. After all how can you do a "bad" job when your team wins it all, and, as I observed at the time, "Who has ever heard a volleyball broadcast on the radio before?"

Then there were the Outhouse Races.

The Indiana County Fair began promoting these strange

competitions in 1995, when Ken Mentch was the Fair Director in charge. Since I did virtually all of the announcing at the fair, I was asked to call the races, and because they were basically a fun event, I knew it wouldn't be too difficult to do.

OUTHOUSE RACE
Before I call an outhouse race, I have to make sure the outhouses are lined up properly before I intone "Get ready, get set, GO!"

Competitors pushed an outhouse on wheels, containing a rider who sat on the "throne" inside the makeshift contraption, down the racetrack around a barrel and back up the track to the finish line.

I used a portable mike and broadcast the races right from the track on the fair's P.A. system. That enabled me to talk to the pushers, and the rider before the race, and get instant reaction when the race was over.

I would make sure the two outhouses were positioned at the starting line so neither had an advantage; then it was "Get ready, get set," pause and wait for Sheriff Bob Fyock to fire the starting pistol, then "Go!"

Many times as the outhouses neared the finish line, after they had gone down the track and circled the barrel, one of the outhouses would careen out of control and I had to be alert to escape without getting hit by an outhouse. Fortunately, so far, I never have.

The races have become a mainstay at the fair every year and since I continue to do the announcing at the fair I will no doubt continue to call the outhouse races each year.

___

So where is all this going?

Well, in 2005 at Duquesne University's annual media day prior to the start of the men's and women's basketball season, Nicole Sinclair, a junior at Duquesne who had played at Indiana High School, was being interviewed by a reporter. I hung around waiting for the interview to end because I had never met Nicole before, and after all, she was a fellow "townie."

When she was finished with the interview, I approached her, saying, "Nicole, I'm Ray Goss. I broadcast the Duquesne men's basketball games, and I'm from Indiana."

Nicole responded enthusiastically. "Ray, I know who you are, you do the outhouse races at the Indiana County Fair. I was a pusher for two years and you interviewed me on the track before the races."

I couldn't stop laughing.

After all the basketball, football, and baseball games I have done in places like Madison Square Garden in New York City and the Los Angeles Coliseum, I guess my tombstone will read "Ray Goss 1937– 'Voice of the Outhouse Races at the Indiana County Fair.'"

NICOLE SINCLAIR
Indiana High School and Duquesne University basketball star who when I met her remembered me as the person who called the "Outhouse Races" at the Indiana County Fair. She had been one of the pushers of an outhouse!

35

TALK ABOUT HECTIC

I was sitting at the computer working on this book at 2:15 p.m. on May 31 2005, when I decided to take a break. My cell phone was on the desk and it was set on "vibrate," which was not unusual because I generally wear it on my belt.

JOHN DEFEO
The ace salesman for WTYM, Kittanning, PA. He's the one who is responsible for my doing volleyball, soccer, and hockey, sports I had never broadcast before. I've told him, "You could sell ice water to Eskimos."

As I picked it up I noticed there was a voice mail message, which meant I had missed a call because I didn't have it on "ring." It turned out that the call was from John DeFeo at WTYM in Kittanning, who was reminding me of a game I had to broadcast at four p. m. today.

TODAY! How can that be? I wondered. John and I had talked about the possibility of a girls' softball game today, but that had been Friday morning and he had said he would try to sell enough ads to justify broadcasting the game, but had indicated if he didn't call me, obviously we wouldn't be broadcasting the game. Now he's saying on the voice mail that we're carrying the game and it's 2:15 and the game starts at 4:00 and Brookville, the site of the game is at least an hour away?

I quickly collected my broadcast equipment and since the game would be tape-recorded for later airing, that took only a few minutes. I rushed downstairs, asked my wife Dee to fill a bottle of water for me, grabbed my cell phone and John's home phone number (since that's where he had called from), and bolted for the car. Before leaving,

I loaded the folding chair and a small portable table that I use for baseball and softball games.

As soon as I pulled out the driveway I called John and after a short discussion on who was supposed to call whom about the game, I said "Never mind, John. It doesn't matter. Just tell me where I'm going and who's playing."

John proceeded to explain that the potential softball game in Brookville had been played earlier and that he had sold the District IX baseball semi-final play-off game between Brookville and Karns City at Karns City. So that meant I wasn't heading to Brookville to do a girls' softball game but to Karns City to broadcast a boys' baseball game. Fortunately, because both are in the same direction, I was on the right road to start with.

"John, how do I get to Karns City? I know I've been there before but what road do I take from Kittanning?"

"Route 268 north from Kittanning and Karns City High School is right on 268."

"Okay, but do you know whether Karns City plays its baseball games right at the school?" That was my next question.

"I'm not sure," John replied. "I think they may play in Parker."

"Parker? Where's Parker?"

"Like I said, Ray, I'm not sure whether they play there or somewhere else. You're going to have to call the school." Then John gave me a number he thought was the correct one for Karns City High School.

I scribbled it down while driving and holding the cell phone, not the ideal safe-driving situation.

I promptly called the number and found that indeed it was the correct one, but of course the Athletic Director, Tom Wagner, whom I knew, wasn't there. He would be at the game site already. I fully anticipated getting a recorded message from the athletic director's office, but instead a secretary picked up the phone.

When I asked her where the game was, she said it was in Fairview, and to my question of "Where's Fairview?" she proceeded to give me directions to the field, which I scribbled down on the back of an envelope, balancing the cell phone between my right shoulder and my ear, and of course also trying to keep an eye on the road.

I also made a mental note to make sure from now on to take my little digital tape recorder with me at all times for situations just like this, so that I could dictate the directions into the machine rather than risk life and limb trying to write while talking on the cell phone and keeping the car on the road.

And then the secretary told me the best news I could possibly hear. When I asked her the starting time of the game, she said 4:30.

Wow, I thought, *that gives me another half-hour.* All the games I've been doing recently had started at four or shortly after school, but, hey, 4:30 is great by me.

Of course I would normally have done at least a half-hour's preparation at home prior to starting for the game, but I didn't have that luxury and would still have to hustle and get line ups, subs, records, etc. when I got there. But that half-hour cushion would really help if I didn't get lost!

It turned out the directions I received were excellent and, more importantly, I could read my chicken-scratch notes that told me what landmarks to look for and whether to turn right or left.

I arrived at the field at 3:40 p. m. and began quickly to get the line ups and other information I needed to make it sound as if I had covered both these teams all season when in fact it was the first time I had seen either one of them.

I discovered the reason the game was scheduled a half-hour later than usual was that two of the three umpires couldn't get there until 4:30. Thank goodness for umpires who have jobs they can't leave at their convenience.

It turned out to be a pleasant day with the sun shining. And, happily, the game was a tightly contested one with Brookville upsetting the number one seed in District 1X, 3–1, to advance to the championship game in the district.

It was a much more relaxed drive back to Kittanning after the game to drop off the tape of the game for re-broadcast the next day.

It's amazing, I thought, as I drove from Kittanning back home to Indiana, *I started broadcasting games 50 years ago and this is the first time that I left for a game without knowing exactly where the game was, when it started, who was playing, and whether it was softball or baseball.*

But then again, this book is titled "Misadventures in Broadcasting" and this experience certainly qualifies.

36

INDIANA'S GOSS HEARD FAR AND WIDE

Editor's note: The following article appeared in The Indiana Gazette on June 23, 1987 and is reprinted courtesy of The Indiana Gazette.

Which Western Pennsylvania sports announcer is heard by more people than anyone else?

Is it Myron Cope, Bill Hillgrove, Lanny Frattare, John Sanders? Would you believe none of the above?

The correct answer is Ray Goss.

Yes, the Ray Goss who broadcasts Duquesne University basketball and lives in Indiana. And not only does Goss have the largest audience, he's heard by more people daily than all of the above sports announcers combined.

How is that possible?

Each morning at 7:20 Monday through Friday, Goss does the sports for Satellite Music Network, and that sportscast is heard on nearly 200 radio stations throughout the United States and places like Bermuda, the British West Indies, Hawaii, and Alaska.

This all started in April when Robert G. Hall, vice president of programming for Satellite Music Network, called Goss at his Homer City Station, STEREO 1160, and asked him to do the morning sports on the Bob Leonard Show.

"Between Robert and Bob, they talked me into giving it a try," Goss said. "It means I have to get up a little earlier, but I enjoy it, and they tell me they're pleased with what I've been doing. In fact, they're trying to talk me into doing two sportscasts a morning," Goss reports. So far he has resisted.

Another interesting fact is that Goss has never met either Hall or Leonard, the men responsible for his doing the sports.

"True, but I've talked to them often enough over the past three years I feel we all know each other pretty well," says Goss.

Since STEREO 1160 is one of the stations using the programming service of Satellite Music Network, there's plenty of opportunity for contact between the station and the network.

Ray Goss, wearing pajamas, is shown doing his morning broadcast from home on Satellite Music Network.

"They encourage suggestions and criticism from their affiliates, and I've never been known to be reluctant to speak up," Goss quipped.

Especially when it comes to sports. Goss offered various suggestions and the network came to look upon and call on Goss for his ideas regarding their handling of sports.

Then came the call with the offer.

"In a nice way they said, 'Okay, you've been telling us how we should do sports, here's your chance to show us,' is the way they put it," said Goss.

What he does is put together as much of the sports he can cram into roughly 75 seconds each morning. And he does it from home.

Between six and seven a.m. he watches at least two TV sportscasts and monitors three others on radio. He has notes from the night before and a schedule of the major events he wants to make sure he covers. How can this be done in 75 seconds?

"I talk real fast," Goss joked.

What he actually does is highlight a major event like an NBA playoff game or the Brewers' 13-game winning streak. Then he notes winners of other games, many times eliminating the time-consuming scores. Goss likes alliteration and tries to end with something, if not humorous, at least offbeat, for his comment or prediction.

Here's a sample of the Goss style: "The bruised and battered Boston Celtics bested the Bucks...the Cards' win catapulted them percentage points past the Cubs...Super Bowl XXV will be played in Tampa in 1991. 1991? Can you imagine planning that far ahead? I don't even know what I'm going to wear this morning."

When the Brewers won 13 straight and were the toast of baseball, then lost 12 in a row, Goss commented, "I guess yesterday's toast just makes today's crumbs," and he correctly predicted the winner of the Boston Marathon by simply saying "watch Seko." (Pronounced Seiko, like the watch. Get it?)

"The technology of all this is rather amazing when you think about it," Goss mused.

From Chicago, Bob Leonard calls Goss at home at approximately 7:15 each morning. On a regular phone from a small office in his home, Goss waits for Leonard's usually offbeat introduction, does his 75-second bit, and throws it back to Bob Leonard.

Meanwhile, the phone call goes through the satellite equipment in Chicago, where Leonard originates his show, through a transponder to Westar 5, a satellite 26,000 miles in orbit above the earth, back to nearly 200 stations affiliated with Satellite Music Network, then through each station's transmitting equipment, into radios throughout the U. S. and beyond.

This all takes 219 milliseconds. How long is that? Goss says, "It sounds like a quick echo, real quick."

And how many people are hearing his morning sports? "Gee, I have no idea," Goss said. "Most of the stations are in smaller markets, like ours, but there are affiliates in major markets or their suburbs like Cincinnati, Minneapolis, San Francisco, Las Vegas, Richmond, Atlanta, Louisville, Indianapolis, Detroit, Tampa, Buffalo, and Milwaukee."

And that's how it's possible for Ray Goss, speaking on a phone from his home in Indiana to have more listeners than any other western Pennsylvania sports announcer.

Postscript: *The Indiana Gazette* doesn't identify the author of this article. Hmm, I wonder who it was?

37

CHECKMATE

I started playing chess when I was a youngster in the junior high grades. That was a long time ago. Now I can't even remember who or what excited my interest in the game. But once I started playing, the competitive juices began to flow, and from my first game I earnestly determined to get better so that I could compete with whoever was across the board from me.

I have memories of study hall in high school when I would make my move on a small, portable, peg board chess set and then, making certain the teacher who was overseeing the study hall, wasn't watching, would pass the board on to my opponent so that he could respond.

Study hall provided a lot of opportunities to play chess. But occasionally the chess games moved into the busy classroom. It wasn't a regular thing, but when the class became really boring or the teacher wasn't paying too much attention, either a classmate or I would communicate with a "Psst, want to play a game?" And the miniature chess board would appear. Of course when passing the board back and forth we had to be ever so much more careful than when operating in the study hall; but I don't remember now that we were ever detected (I'm sure there would have been a commotion.).

Later, when I started to broadcast intercollegiate athletic events, and was thus spending many hours on the road, chess became a welcome pastime. Two people with whom I especially enjoyed playing chess were a fellow broadcaster and a basketball player.

John Cigna provided the color commentary for the Duquesne basketball broadcasts in 1971, and when each of us discovered that the other played chess, the road trips were consumed with nearly non-stop games.

John could best be described as aggressive, and he would probably report the same of me. I recall that when we started working together I had told him, "John, I know it's tough to do 'color' because I'm talking most of the time describing the action. But I want you to jump in whenever you want, as long as there's a brief lull in the action. And since there's no way for me to know when you want to say something, just tap me on the arm and I'll shut up."

I've worked with many "color" commentators, and I have always given the above directions to each of them. Most of them forgot to do it at all, and some were so tentative in tapping me that I sometimes felt nothing. Not John. He would whack me on the arm so that there could be no doubt that he wanted to say something. After a few blows suffered in the first game that we worked together, I said (during a break for a commercial), "John, it's okay to tap me, but my arm is really sore from the pounding I'm taking from you."

He promptly apologized: "Sorry, Ray, but you know I was raised in Brooklyn where you had to fight for every breath of air; so I'm naturally a little aggressive." "Little!" I replied, "My arm is going to be black and blue before the game is over."

I think he let up just a bit after that, but you get the idea, and after one year of doing "color" on the games, John got his big break in Pittsburgh radio when he was hired by KDKA. After beginning as a night-time talk-show host, he took over the prestigious "morning-drive" time spot on KDKA and went on to become a household name in the Pittsburgh area.

But back to the chess. John and I would play anywhere and everywhere. Certainly on planes and busses, and in our hotel rooms. I vividly remember the time when we were traveling by taxi in New York City on a fast and bumpy, wild ride through a bewildering succession of congested intersections. At the time we engaged the cab, John was ahead in the game. But after the careening ride, that tested not only our ability to concentrate on the chess match but our ability to balance the miniature board so that the pieces didn't go flying all over the cab, we emerged from the taxi to discover that I had taken a decisive advantage in the game. Naturally John complained: "That's not fair. That cab was bouncing all over the place. You can't count moves that were made in a whirlpool."

My response was simple. "John, I was riding in the same cab as you."

Another match that I remember occurred while we were returning from a road game and getting off the plane in Pittsburgh. As we walked through the airport terminal side by side we were still in the midst of a hotly contested match. After making a move I handed the chess set to John and said, "John, I have to hit the men's room."

He accepted the chess board to ponder his move, while noting, "I have to go too."

As we approached the men's room, he made his move, and handed me the set. As we faced adjoining urinals, I made my move and handed the set back to John.

Now as I look back on all of this I can only imagine what the curious onlookers must have been thinking.

During the years I played lots of matches in truly absurd conditions. One that I'll never forget found me pitted against a very popular basketball player.

Mel Hankinson was a sophomore at Indiana State College (later Indiana University of Pennsylvania, or more simply IUP) when I discovered he liked to play chess.

Mel not only went on to become an outstanding college basketball player but a successful coach who authored books about the game of basketball and even served as a consultant on Hollywood movies that had basketball themes.

Mel still holds the individual single-game scoring record at IUP, 59 points versus Parsons College of Iowa, tallied in a game I was privileged to broadcast.

And of course Mel was very competitive when it came to chess.

We played many times on the bus as the team journeyed to road games at such exotic locales as Clarion, Slippery Rock, Lock Haven, and Shippensburg.

Early in his sophomore year, Mel was advised by veteran IUP

Coach Peck McKnight that he would be starting his first game in a conference clash at Edinboro.

Edinboro, back then before I-79, was a good three-hour bus ride from Indiana. Shortly after boarding the bus, Mel and I started playing chess. We completed two games before we arrived in Edinboro, three hours before game time. Arrangements had been made for the team's pre-game meal at the Edinboro cafeteria; so Mel and I with chess board in hand proceeded through the cafeteria line and sat next to each other to pick away at our dinners all the while moving the rook or the knight to some advantageous position.

By the time dinner had ended, our game had reached a climactic point. Ever resourceful, Mel suggested that we adjourn to the nearby school library in order to finish the game. He noted that there were yet two hours before game time. "We've got plenty of time," he said.

But the game lasted longer than either of us had anticipated, and I remember that after I checked my watch, I observed to Mel, "We had better continue this later. You need to get dressed for the game and I need to hook up my equipment." Of course I was more concerned about Mel, because this would be his first game as a starter, and I didn't want him to jeopardize that opportunity.

Mel countered with, "Just a few more moves and we should be finished."

Well, when you start concentrating deeply on what move you should be making, time can fly by more quickly than you could ever imagine. Finally the game was over, and because I honestly can not remember who won the match, Mel must have. Or maybe we even agreed on a draw. Anyhow, by the time we started to hustle for the field house, we noted that it was very close to game time.

Waiting for us at the door to the building stood an irate Coach Peck McKnight.

I can't remember exactly the language of his "colorful" greeting. Suffice to say it was not cordial. And after he finished ripping into Mel, and informing him in no uncertain terms that not only was he not starting but that he might not even play, he turned to address me.

"And you, Goss, you're older. I thought you would know better. Playing chess with one of my players who should be thinking only about basketball." I'm not sure what I replied. I think I thought about suggesting that at least I was teaching his basketball player how to concentrate intently on what he was doing. But I know I didn't actually say that. I believe I mumbled something like "I'm sorry, coach, it won't happen again."

And it never did, because Mel and I never played chess again.

38

MUSICAL CHAIRS

The day before the 1972 Duquesne basketball season was set to begin I received a phone call from the program director of Radio Station KDKA.

Since WJAS, the NBC owned and operated station, had been sold and the format changed, it was deemed that basketball didn't fit in with their programming philosophy. Amazingly, a deal was struck with KDKA to air the Duquesne games. Now anyone who knows anything about broadcasting history knows that KDKA was the first radio station in the United States and, with 50,000 watts of power, it remains one of the premier radio stations in the country.

After the program director introduced himself, he immediately apologized. No one had been selected to do the color commentary on the Duquesne broadcasts, and he was calling to get my reaction to some of the people they were considering. One of the names he mentioned was Dave Fabilli. He wanted to know what I thought about him and his work. I told him I knew Dave because he had sat behind me at Duquesne home games the past two years doing the play-by-play for Duquesne's student radio station WDUQ, the same thing I had done in the mid-fifties. But I had to admit I had never actually heard him on the air because I was broadcasting the same game he was at the same time.

The program director concluded our conversation by saying he would get back to me later that day or early the next day to let me know whom they had selected to work with me. I remember telling him, "That's okay, I'm coming down for the game anyway, so it doesn't matter who it is."

And the next day I drove to Pittsburgh not knowing who or whether anyone would be working with me on the first game of the season. Well, it turned out to be Dave Fabilli. And naturally for the first game he was understandably a bit nervous. To come out of college and start out by being on prestigious and powerful KDKA can be a little unnerving to a veteran, let alone a neophyte.

At one point, during a commercial break, Dave asked me whether he could "break the station" at the top of the hour. It's a broadcast requirement to identify the station's location and call letters once an hour near the top of the hour and Dave wanted that privilege. "No problem," I said.

Dave worked three or four games with me before KDKA decided that perhaps he wasn't the right person. My broadcast style, especially with basketball, is pretty much non-stop talking. There's so much going on and I attempt to let the listener know as much as possible. That means the "color" guy has to be pretty aggressive to get in a word here or there. I always try to pause when there's a momentary break in the action to give my broadcast partner an opportunity to jump in with a comment, but in defense of Dave, who had never worked with me, it had to be difficult to anticipate when to come in and when not to.

My next broadcast partner that year was Chuck Cooper, the legendary Duquesne player from the late '40s who was the

CHUCK COOPER
Duquesne All–America, signed by the Boston Celtics in 1950, the first black player to receive a contract to play in the NBA.

first black player signed to an NBA contract when the Boston Celtics made him their first-round pick in 1950.

Chuck had never worked in radio before and after two games he was the one who decided it wasn't for him.

Next came Bill Griever. Bill worked for the Louis Sautel Agency, the producer of the Duquesne games at the time. Bill helped sell some of the advertisers and expressed an interest in working the games. Again, though, he had had little or no previous broadcast experience; and after three or four games, that was it for Bill.

That's when I became involved. I called the program director at KDKA and told him I had done many games over the years by myself and would prefer to do the rest of the games without any "help." He agreed and I flew solo the rest of the season, which was certainly easier than wondering who would be showing up next.

From not knowing whom I would be working with when I showed up for the first game, to working with three different people, to flying solo, Duquesne's only year on KDKA, one of America's most powerful and prestigious radio stations, turned out to be the broadcast version of "musical chairs."

39

DES MOINES TO PITTSBURGH BY BUS

We were scheduled to depart by bus at 5:30 a.m., Sunday, Dec. 2, 2007 in order to arrive at the Des Moines Airport for our flight to Chicago en route to Pittsburgh.

Duquesne University on the night before had lost to the host Drake Bulldogs in the finals of the Iowa Realty Basketball Tournament. It was a tough 77–73 defeat, the Dukes' first loss after six season-opening wins.

My broadcast partner and roommate George Von Benko, as is his custom, was awake at 3:30 a.m. two hours before our scheduled departure. He wanted to make sure he was ready on time.

GEORGE VON BENKO
My partner on the Duquesne basketball broadcasts since 2000. George amazes me with the breadth and depth of his sports knowledge. And when it comes to discussing movies, music, and history, his recall of facts and details is astounding.

It had been a "short" night because it had been well after midnight following the game before we "hit the sack."

Even though he seems to be rising a whole hour before he needs to, I don't really mind that George gets up so early. I don't understand it, but I don't mind it. After all, that means the bathroom will be available when I roll out at the more respectable hour of 4:30 a.m.

It's not that George requires nearly two hours to shower, shave, pack, etc. to get ready to leave. In fact, George is dressed and ready to go at least forty-five minutes before departure time. In this case, he was ready to go at 4:45 a.m., and had fallen into his routine, which means reclining in a chair and falling asleep until it's time to leave the

179

room and get on the bus. Why he does this is beyond me, but George is George, and I'm sure he wonders why I get up so late.

At any rate, George and I, together with some of the players, were on the bus at 5:20 a.m. when Assistant Coach Bill Barton walked onto the bus with a startling announcement: "Our flight to Chicago has been cancelled. Get your keys back and go to your rooms and get some sleep. We'll call you when we figure out what we're doing."

Because of the snow and ice storms that had hit our area we should have expected the cancellation. We knew all about Chicago.

So it was back to our room and back to bed. Now have you ever tried to sleep in a situation like that? No way. Then around seven a.m. the phone rang with the news that in fifteen minutes or so we would be leaving by bus.

By bus? It's nearly 800 miles from Des Moines to Pittsburgh. Still, when we thought about it, the bus trip seemed maybe better than waiting around at the airport.

At about 7:30 a.m. the bus pulled out. One good move was made when the Duquesne team managers visited the nearby McDonald's restaurant and came back with an assortment of breakfast sandwiches, orange juice, etc. That sure saved some valuable time. Can you picture all twenty-five of us lining up to order individually and how long that would take?

The bus driver had to make one stop before starting east, and that was to pick up another driver. A trip of this length needed two drivers to alternate because of the rule limiting the number of hours one driver can drive in one day. The estimate we were hearing was that it would take 12 to 13 hours to get to Pittsburgh. I immediately figured, *Yeah, if we don't stop to eat,* which I knew we would.

Even though the rain was pelting down steadily, we all appreciated that rain was better than snow. After we picked up the other driver, we hit the open road. As the miles rolled by I alternated between cat naps and reading the latest John Grisham novel, *The Innocent Man.*

Somewhere around one p.m. we pulled off the interstate for lunch. Each of was handed $10, and, fortunately, there were four or five fast-food restaurants that beckoned. Coach Ron Everhart said, "Grab it and go. We want to be on our way in twenty minutes." Of course that never happened. With a handful of players, I decided on Taco Bell, and about 45 minutes later, not 20, we were on our way again.

The afternoon hours dragged on, but as darkness began to fall we found ourselves near Columbus, Ohio, on route 70. It was time for dinner. That meant another $10, thank you, and four or five more fast-food restaurants to tempt our palates. I chose Boston Market this time and was happy to discover the chicken pot pie "okay."

Since the bus trip was unplanned, we didn't have the normal supply of movies aboard. Luckily it just so happened that near our latest stop there appeared a video store and assistant coach Bill Barton and Director of Basketball Operations Jason Byrd departed to make the crucial decisions on which movies to choose. I think Jason went along to represent the players since he's in his mid-twenties and Bill is forty-seven.

They were back in ten minutes or so and we began to watch the first of what turned out to be four back-to-back movies.

That's when it happened!

We were somewhere east of Columbus and west of Zanesville, Ohio, when a loud BANG caused everyone on the bus to jump almost out of his seat. All exclaimed together, "What was that?"

The bus driver having pulled over to the shoulder of the road, a couple of the players on the left side of the bus were able to report that a two-door sports car had hydroplaned on the wet pavement and smashed into the side of the bus.

Fortunately the lady driving the car was not injured. Of course we knew it would be some time before the police would arrive and we could get on our way again.

In fact, it was an hour and a half before we were able to continue. A luggage compartment on the left side of the bus had been smashed in but when a car tangles with a bus, the loser is obvious, and the lady's car was smashed both front and rear. It seems that when she hydroplaned on the wet road the car rammed the medial strip to her left and was propelled backward into the bus, thus damaging the rear of her car.

She was indeed fortunate to be uninjured. Vic Bauer, the Duquesne trainer, who had checked her out, was happy to report that she had suffered nothing more than "abrasions" to her knees.

Although the evening hours dragged on wearily, they were made tolerable by the films and by the sophisticated cell phones carried by some of the players. Somehow somebody was able to discover from time to time the score of the Steelers–Bengals game, which I had certainly expected to view at home.

Long before the bus pulled into Palumbo Center (which was at one a. m. Monday morning) we had the good news that after falling behind 7-0, the Steelers had outlasted the Bengals and had posted a 24-14 win.

After gathering up my luggage, and making my way to the parking garage, I drove the fifty-nine miles home to Indiana, Pa. My head finally hit the pillow at 2:30 a.m.

We had lost an hour coming east, for actually the departure time of 7:30 a.m. in Des Moines was 8:30 Eastern time. Since we arrived at one a.m. the next day, the bus trip required sixteen and one-half-hours!

One of the benefits of retirement is that one does not have to get up early on Monday morning for work. No matter, I was still awake, wide awake before seven a.m. At least I would have a whole day to recover from the longest bus ride I've ever experienced.

When I think of this trip, I'm reminded of all those times over the years when people, discovering that I broadcast the Duquesne basketball games on the radio, invariably ask: "Do you go with the team on the road trips?" When I answer in the affirmative, their faces really light up. It's an envious expression that I take to mean "Boy, are you lucky."

Yeah.

40

HOLE-Y MOLEY

The Duquesne Dukes flew into New York City on February 19, 1971, and were promptly bused to their rooms at the Waldorf–Astoria in the heart of Manhattan in preparation for meeting St. Peter's at Madison Square Garden the next day.

I had just bought a new suit that I would wear for the first time. It was grayish-blue in color with a couple of muted stripes running vertically and I really liked it. It was all wool and I decided that since we were flying right back to Pittsburgh after the Saturday afternoon game I would wear the suit pants on the plane to New York, and then don the suit coat for the game the next day.

When I awakened Saturday morning I noticed in the clothes closet an ironing board and an iron. This discovery led to the realization that my suit pants needed a quick pressing so they would look sharp for the game. Now I'm not the greatest when it comes to ironing clothes. In fact, as I look back on this incident, I don't think I ever pressed a pair of pants before, *but how hard could it be* I thought. I used to watch my Dad press his trousers every Sunday morning before going to church, and if he could do it, I certainly could.

I set up the ironing board and plugged in the iron and waited a few minutes for it to get hot. Then I carefully placed one pant leg on the ironing board and pressed the iron to the fabric. I started to try to move the iron on the trouser leg but it wouldn't budge. It was stuck right where I had placed it. And worse yet, I heard a sizzling sound and the unmistakable odor of burning fabric. I quickly removed the iron from the pants and stared in utter disbelief at a giant hole right there in my new suit pants. I didn't want to believe it, but there it was. How could this have happened? I had hardly touched the pants with the iron. Of course in those days they didn't have settings for various fabrics as they do today, and because the pants were 100% wool, and the iron was very hot, the trousers obviously didn't take kindly to the searing heat.

Panicsville!

What do I do now? It's nearly 11 a. m. and the bus leaves the hotel at noon for the two o'clock game and I don't have another pair of pants to wear. *Maybe the suit coat will cover the hole* I thought as I hurriedly grabbed my coat from the closet. No dice. The hole was actually on the rear of the pants but partway down the right leg and there was no way it wouldn't be visible. Not only that, it was huge.

Then I remembered something. There was a men's store on the ground floor of the hotel. Seizing the phone, I called the front desk, and was quickly put in touch with a salesman from the men's shop. I relayed my tale of woe and asked whether there was any possibility for someone to bring some trousers to my room for a possible sale. I didn't feel I could even wear the pants down to the store. The salesman asked my size and what color slacks I might prefer. I told him blue would probably go best with my suit coat. I also asked him whether he could hurry because I had to check out in less than an hour.

Although it seemed a lot longer, it could have been no more than ten minutes before someone knocked on my hotel door. A salesman appeared with a couple of suggestions. At this point I couldn't afford to be too choosey. I took a pair of blue pants and quickly tried them on right there in front of the salesman. They weren't the greatest. They weren't even wool and, as I remember, they were flared at the bottom. Remember, this was 1971, and I didn't particularly like that. But what option did I have? I purchased the pants with cash right then and there, thanking the salesman for his personal service, giving him a tip, as I recall, and a few minutes later I was dressed, packed, and heading for the team bus.

As I think back on it all now, I believe that what bothers me most is that no one ever noticed the obviously different pair of trousers I had on with my suit coat, or maybe they did notice them and were just being kind and didn't want to mention the strange get-up I was wearing.

41

40 YEARS AND COUNTING

DEE GOSS

Without a doubt, my better half, who has put up with me for 48 years of marriage, and counting. Dee is also the mother of our seven wonderful children.

The 2007–08 basketball season marked the 40th consecutive year that I had broadcast Duquesne basketball on the radio in Pittsburgh.

In a study of the currently active broadcasters of NCAA Division I basketball, it was found that I was in the number four spot nationally for consecutive years broadcasting for the same team, just one year ahead of Bill Hillgrove, the play-by-play man for Pitt basketball. So, in addition to being number four nationally, I guess I'm number one in Pittsburgh, as far as longevity is concerned.

As the basketball season was coming to a close, I received a letter from Duquesne Athletic Director Greg Amodio informing me that Duquesne wanted to recognize my forty years of broadcasting the Dukes' games at halftime of the St. Louis home game on March eighth.

And, I was informed in addition to the recognition I could have as many tickets as needed for family and friends to attend the game. Bob Derda, Associate Athletic Director, didn't even flinch when I told him, about a week before the St. Louis game, that I might need as many as 35 tickets.

"Are you sure that's enough, Ray?" he asked.

When I asked Bob if something could be arranged to feed the people who would be attending the game on my behalf, he promptly arranged a fine reception, food included, in Duquesne President Dr.

Charles Dougherty's special reception suite above the court. I offered to pay for the food, but Bob said that would not be a problem, and that they would simply replenish the food that would be served during a reception in the suite that occurred while the game was being played.

I knew it would be difficult for all seven of our children to attend the game. Our three sons are in Kansas City, Orlando, and Vero Beach, Florida. I called to invite them but said I didn't expect them to come because of the distance and the difficulty in trying to arrange their busy work schedules.

Our four daughters all planned to attend, but at the last minute Lisa's older son Jack, who was born with Down Syndrome, and has experienced many health challenges, awoke on the morning of the game with a fever, and Lisa, rightly so, opted to stay with him.

And because Amy, our youngest daughter, who was expecting her second child, had just come down with the flu, she of course had to stay at home.

Prior the start of the game, while George Von Benko and I were doing the pre-game show, I noticed some activity across the floor from our court-side broadcast position. It was occurring in the section in which my family and friends were sitting. As I studied the rumpus more closely, I noticed that our sons David and Jason were hugging my wife and their sisters Christine and Julie.

I leaned over to Dave Saba, Duquesne's Associate Athletic Director of Media Relations, and said rather excitedly, "How about that? My sons David and Jason just showed up."

Dave replied. "I know. They called for tickets and told us to keep it quiet because they wanted to surprise everyone." Well, they certainly had, and what a great surprise it was!

Later I asked them when it was that they had decided to come. Jason said, "Right after you called, I called David and said, 'Clear your schedule for the weekend of March eighth, we're going to Pittsburgh.'"

Jason also reported that they had hoped to get Tom to come and were sorry to learn that because of his work schedule he would not be able to make it.

Just before tip-off, which was the last home game of the season for Duquesne, the departing three Duquesne seniors were honored. Kieron Achara, Reggie Jackson, and Gary Tucker were introduced to the crowd; and their jerseys, which had been encased in a large frame, were unveiled and presented to them. The crowd stood to applaud and honor their contributions to Duquesne basketball.

My 40-year recognition occurred at halftime. I accompanied Athletic Director Greg Amodio to center court where awaiting on a tripod was something large, covered by a black cloth and looking very similar to the awards the three seniors had received just before the start of the game.

As the Public Address Announcer Bill Fontana read details of my 40 years of broadcasting the Duquesne games, the crowd was standing and applauding.

Then, at the appropriate time, Greg Amodio reached up and pulled off the covering of the frame, revealing a large Duquesne jersey that had "Dukes" inscribed on it with the number "1" underneath. And at the bottom below the jersey were the words "Ray Goss, Voice of the Dukes."

After Greg removed the cover he shook my hand as pictures were being taken. I remember saying to Greg, "You can't give me number one, that's Aaron Jackson's number (Aaron was a junior) and he'll need it next year." I'll never forget Greg's response: "No, Ray, you're number one."

The Dukes went on to win the game over St. Louis 85-58, and the reception afterwards was just terrific. Head Coach Ron Everhart took time to join us and meet the members of my family and the friends who were attending.

GREG AMODIO
Duquesne University Athletic Director Greg Amodio congratulates Ray Goss on his 40th consecutive year of broadcasting Duquesne basketball.

I have many fond memories of Duquesne basketball over the years but certainly right there near the top was the wonderful recognition accorded me on 40 years of broadcasting the games.

42

LOOKING BACK AND AHEAD

MY DAD
Talk about chic! Everything he did he did to perfection. I didn't realize it at the time but he was teaching me that the only way to do a job is to do it right. He was a quiet guy, the epitome of "actions speak louder than words." Thanks, Dad.

As I was writing the various chapters in this book I kept wondering how am I going to end this thing?

Then one day it hit me. It was easy enough recounting the many wild and crazy experiences I had in broadcasting but perhaps the reader would like some type of overview, in other words, what are my thoughts regarding this half century plus of broadcasting and when do I intend to pull the plug if it isn't first pulled on me.

As I thought about these things I couldn't help thinking about my Dad.

He was born in 1903 with the unlikely first name of Felix. And dislike it he did, because as I was growing up I found that no one called him Felix, but rather "Bib." It came from his younger brother who called him Bib because he couldn't say brother.

My father died in 1967 from lung cancer, which was caused by a lifetime of smoking. He worked in a steel mill, Superior Steel, in Carnegie, Pa. all his life until the plant shut down in 1963, one of many to do so in the Pittsburgh area.

What I learned from my Dad didn't come from talks he had with me. Unlike me he wasn't a very vocal person. He had only an eighth grade education, which wasn't uncommon in those days. But his common sense and how he handled the meager finances of our household and took care of our home didn't need vocalizing. His actions spoke volumes and little did I realize at the time that some of his admirable traits were rubbing off. Like how he did things. To say he was a perfectionist would be an understatement.

When he mowed the lawn he would double cut the whole lawn to make sure he didn't miss anything. When I got old enough to "cut the grass," he would watch me and more than once say "You missed some on that last pass. Do it over." Of course I was always trying to finish as fast as I could so that I could get to a ball game that seemed to be always waiting for me.

The hedges were another matter altogether. We had this lovely hedge-type fence that surrounded our yard. And it was the straightest in the whole neighborhood. My Dad used to run string attached to sticks to each end of the hedge. Then he would carefully clip the hedges so they lined up perfectly with the string. And when I got old enough to attempt to cut the hedges, I could never satisfy him because if I goofed and cut too much in one spot, which I invariably did, that would ruin the whole appearance until it would grow in again in a week or two.

As a result, and I wasn't too disappointed in this, I was banned from cutting the hedges. The grass was okay for me to cut because I couldn't ruin it, just miss some spots that my Dad would always dutifully point out and which I would then cut again to make the lawn measure up to his standards.

Without ever saying it, what my Dad taught me about mowing the lawn and cutting the hedges could be encapsulated in the old saying "A job worth doing is worth doing right."

Keeping this in mind, when I started broadcasting games, I would always try to have them tape recorded. Then I could review them afterwards, not to hear how good I sounded, but to listen to all the mistakes I was making and work to eliminate them so that I wouldn't make them again next time.

It wasn't always easy to tape games back in the early '60s shortly after I was first married. Because this was before cassette recorders, I bought a bulky Wollensak reel-to-reel machine, and I would always instruct my wife Dee when to turn on the tape recorder, which was hooked into a radio, so that she could record my broadcast wherever I was.

More than once I'd come home to say, especially after an exciting game, "Did you get the whole game recorded okay?"

And she might say, "Well I missed some of the beginning," or "I forgot to turn the tape over at halftime when I got busy, so I missed the second half." That didn't make me too happy, but fortunately cassette tape recorders came along shortly thereafter. A good thing too, or else our marriage may have come to a screeching halt instead of flourishing as it has for 48 years and counting.

That meant when I started broadcasting the Duquesne basketball games in Pittsburgh in 1968, I was able to tape the action right at the game site. That way I could listen to practically the whole game on my hour and 15 minute ride back home to Indiana, Pa. Besides, if there was an exciting finish to the game, I could re-cue it and play it on our post-game show. Back then there weren't too many people doing that.

When I would listen to tapes of my games, I would always try to put myself in the shoes of the listener. What does he or she want to hear or know immediately? Well it's rather basic. Let's use basketball as an example. The score, the score, always the score, and how much time is left. So over the years I trained myself to give the score not only every time a team scores, but every time a team doesn't score, which even in basketball could mean two or three minutes at times. Besides, I always try to remember to give the score this way: "Duquesne 36, Pitt 34, with 2:14 remaining in the first half." Why this way precisely? Well again as a listener, I know I've tuned in to many games and have not heard the score for two or three minutes and not just because no one was scoring. Sometimes there was scoring you never heard about. Then at times I would hear that the score is now 36 to 34. Great, I just tuned in. Who has the 36, and who has the 34? And then I would hear "With two minutes to go." *Wow*, I would think, *it's really a low-scoring game*, but really the announcer had simply forgotten to say "in the first half."

Details, details, details. But isn't that what you as a listener want? And where did all this come from? From listening to myself on tape numerous times and realizing I was making these kinds of mistakes and then trying to be sure not to repeat them. And there's only one place I learned this, from the disciplined, painstaking way my Dad did any kind of work around the house, the lawn and hedges just being two examples.

Then when I look back, I wonder how did I ever get interested in sports in the first place? The answer, no surprise, is, well, from my Dad again.

I can recall seeing my first Pittsburgh Pirate baseball game at Forbes Field when I was five years old. My Dad would take me two or three times a year. I'm sure it would have been more often if he could have afforded to do so, but boy did I ever enjoy those trips, and look forward to them. Then of course we would listen to the games on the radio when "Rosey" Rosewell was the "Voice of the Pirates."

Because baseball was my Dad's first love, it became mine. Football was next and we would go to the local Scott Township High School football games and even a Pittsburgh Steelers game now and then. My childhood revolved around sports, either watching or listening to games or playing sports.

My Mother once complained to my Dad by saying, "All he wants to do is play ball."

My Dad reassured her by saying, "That's okay; it keeps him out of trouble."

The more I played the more I dreamed of being either a Pittsburgh Pirate or later when I was introduced to the game of basketball in junior high a pro in the NBA.

But high school sports put a damper on those dreams. I was on the Scott Township baseball and basketball teams, but not only didn't I start, even in my senior year, I rarely got into the games at all. That's when I began wondering how else could I be involved in sports, and broadcasting games seemed like the next best thing. And you know what, it has been, for over 50 years now.

Whether it's a Little League baseball game, and I've done my share of those, or an NCAA playoff game at one of the nation's top arenas, I still enjoy what I do. So it doesn't feel like work and, as I look ahead, I intend to keep doing what I'm doing. In fact it's even more enjoyable now. When I began doing games commercially at age 21, it was always in addition to my full-time job in radio, first as an announcer, then newsman, followed by sales, then management, and finally co-owner of a radio station. Those were my full-time jobs and sports broadcasting was like a part-time second job. But for the last 20 years I have not worked full-time, just part time doing sports broadcasting. What could be better? There's more time to prepare for the games, when one does not have to be constantly concerned about a full-time job.

So in looking ahead I expect to continue to do what I'm doing, roughly 60 to 70 sporting events a year or even more, if the opportunity presents itself.

When someone asks me about retiring completely my standard response is I hope I'll know when it's time to quit, either because I'll get tired of broadcasting games (I doubt it) or I realize that my broadcasts just don't measure up to the standards I've established, and it's all because my Dad, probably without ever being aware of it, taught me that "A job worth doing is a job worth doing right."

ACKNOWLEDGMENTS

Thanks, first of all, to all of the people you read about in this book. If it weren't for them, the experiences I've had the past 50 plus years broadcasting sports would certainly have been much less enjoyable.

I talked to many of these people who have much better memories than I do. And they were able to supply facts and details that enhanced many of the stories.

Perhaps my favorite was Jack Benedict's line on the "Air Benedict" chapter when I asked him if he remembered the exact date of our nearly ill-fated flight. Without hesitation he replied, "November 18, 1989. I can still see it on my tombstone."

In the introduction to this book, I wrote about how much my good friend Bill Betts has meant to me when it came to every aspect of this book. I just wanted to acknowledge him again for his tireless efforts on my behalf.

John Katshir, a good friend and the best man at my wedding, was instrumental in making certain this book would be published.

Both my sister, Felicia Ragazzo, and my good friend Mary Ann Pflumm proof-read and spotted many misspellings and grammatical errors, thus helping to keep the errors to a minimum.

Thanks also to my son-in-law Rob Brownlee, a graphic artist, who designed the front and back covers of the book, and to Dave DeNoma, the Duquesne University photographer, who snapped the picture that appears on the front cover.

And then there's my wife Dee, who, patiently and without complaining, has been hearing about this book for years, because, actually, the first couple of chapters were written several years ago. Then there were months when I didn't write anything, followed by spurts of writing. This happened again and again. Dee is probably happier than I am that the book finally has been published.

And last, but certainly not least, thanks to you, dear reader. I wanted this book to be a collection of zany incidents that might amuse you and perhaps give you a little better insight into what can happen to someone who's spent a lifetime broadcasting sports.

I hope you have enjoyed reading about these experiences.

INDEX